Ebenezer Mudgett
and the
Pine Tree Riot

EBENEZER MUDGETT
and the
PINE TREE RIOT

Connie Evans

Copyright © 2017 Connie Evans
Print Edition

All rights reserved. No part of this publication may be reproduced, distributed, or transmitted in any form or by any means, including photocopying, recording, or other electronic or mechanical methods, without the prior written permission of the publisher, except in the case of brief quotations embodied in critical reviews and certain other noncommercial uses permitted by copyright law.

Table of Contents

Preface	xi
1. The King's Broad Arrow	1
2. Quimby's Inn	10
3. The Journey's Preparation	20
4. The Farewell	29
5. The Journey Begins	34
6. An Unfortunate Encounter	45
7. The Goat's Head Tavern to the Merrimack River	53
8. A Seed is Planted	62
9. A Conversation Begins	73
10. An Unwelcome Visitor	81
11. Homeward Bound	92
12. The River Bend Inn	102
13. The Homecoming	111
14. The Reckoning	119
15. Representation	126
16. Resistance Brews	133
17. A Warrant Is Served	141
18. The Pine Tree Riot	151

19. Retribution Expected	162
20. September 8, 1772	172
Afterword	178
Glossary	182

Acknowledgment

I am very grateful for the help I received along this journey of discovery. Fortunately, I joined The Weare Area Writers Group when I began to write about Ebenezer and the Pine Tree Riot. I have learned a lot about writing by listening to their work. The members gave me the encouragement I needed to continue fleshing out the people and events of 1772. Thank you to Sharon Czarnecki for her cheerleading and leadership; Jennifer Wallace for her immeasurable help with the publishing process; Tom Clow and Stephen Wallace for refining my subtitle; Ellen Reed, Marge Burke, Frank Oehischlaeger and Bob Jarvis for their constructive critiques. My husband, Gary, gave me insightful commentaries for each chapter, and I found his honesty invaluable. Two local historians, Betty Straw and Sylvia Beaupre, graciously accepted my request to read the manuscript and check for historical accuracy. Arnold Rocklin-Weare was helpful in meeting with me to discuss Ebenezer and the house where the Mudgetts lived and where the eight men involved in the Pine Tree Riot conceived the plan for their notorious offense.

This book would not have been possible without the major assistance of *The History of Weare, New Hampshire 1735-1888* by William Little and the Town

Committee who furnished the material in 1888. It was through their undertaking that inspired me to dig deeper and research life in the 1770s.

Liberty has never come from the government. Liberty has always come from subjects of the government. The history of government is a history of resistance.

—Woodrow Wilson

Preface

In many ways, most of the 18th century was not an auspicious time in America. The New World was under the watchful eye of King George III by means of his abettors: the governors he had chosen and their underlings. The increase in laws and taxes heaped on the colonists was beginning to reach a breaking point, forcing good, law-abiding men to make audacious decisions. At the same time, these men were endeavoring to carve out an existence for themselves in a hardscrabble environment that would challenge even the hardiest of modern men.

Merely fifteen years before the story begins, much of the area was described as a howling wilderness. Neighbors were scarce then, unless one counted the wolves, wildcats, bears, beavers, and foxes, as well as Indians, who were well-known to remove one's scalp with little, if any, provocation. The few brave pioneers who chose to settle in the virgin forests had to mark the trees to find their way back home—or wander around lost. The simple tools available to create their dominion over nature required strong backs and the full measure of their strength.

Even so, the area had a lot to offer the early settlers. They were attracted to the many ponds, streams, and the Piscataquog River that crisscrosses the land, the latter being an Indian name that translates as *place of many deer*. The fast-flowing river not only provided fish and attracted animals to trap and hunt but served as transportation for man and merchandise in the deeper spots. Meadows broke up the forests, and the hills provided good vantage points.

Travel remained a challenge throughout the 18th century. Enterprises, such as Ebenezer Mudgett's trade in spiritous liquors, required up to a two-week journey in the dead of winter to replenish supplies. The easiest form of travel was to hitch a team of oxen, more rugged and hardier than horses, to a sled with high sides, called a pung, and slide along the rough, snow-packed trails. More than one man froze to death en route.

Before Weare was settled, many men from the surrounding area participated in the French and Indian War. The war stemmed from a boundary dispute over who owned the Ohio Valley. King George had sent surveyors to lay out the six hundred thousand acres to the Ohio Company and to trade with the Indians. The French either put the surveyors in prison or drove them out. Meanwhile, the Indians began to murder the settlers on the frontier, burn their houses, and carry captives to Canada. New Hampshire also experienced the wrath of the Indians and received the same treatment. England sent soldiers to aid in defending the settlers; a few of these settlers would move to Weare when the war ended in 1763.

Ebenezer Mudgett and his wife, Miriam, moved their family to Weare in 1765, three years after King George III changed the name from Robiestown to Wearetown, after Meshech Weare, a New Hampshire statesman. Eventually, people simply referred to the town as Weare. The money Ebenezer earned as a liquor merchant afforded him the opportunity to buy a house from Jeremiah Allen for £5,600. It was across from Aaron Quimby's Inn, which plays an important role in our story. Such a grand sum of money in 1765 affirmed Ebenezer as one of the wealthiest, if not *the* wealthiest man in town.

When the French and Indian War ended in 1763, an influx of settlers arrived in what is now called Weare, and Ebenezer's business acumen told him it was wise to get a foothold in the burgeoning hamlet. There were already three taverns in the town by 1765, indicating the settlers' heightened thirst for spirits would support his growing family as well as keep him busy supplying his homemade ale and apple jack. To augment his own brews, he sold some fine West Indies rum in Weare and other nearby New Hampshire towns. He knew that spirits had a way of turning a tidy profit, as long as he could keep them stocked, which accounted for his many forays southward to Salem, home to one of the fifty-one rum distilleries at that time in Massachusetts.

In 1690 King William and Queen Mary established the Pine Tree Law that would start to have its full effect on the settlements in New Hampshire in 1766.

The law required that any white pine tree with a minimum diameter of twelve inches became the King's property and was to be marked with a symbol called the King's Broad Arrow. A fine from £5 to £50, depending on the diameter of the tree, was imposed if anyone dared to saw one down. If the offender did not pay the fine, he was thrown in prison, his release determined at the will of His Majesty's officers. Furthermore, the despised law required a fee for a license on the smaller trees.

When Weare received the charter for the town from King George III in 1764, the King included the Pine Tree Law in the charter. It had not been rigorously enforced until Governor John Wentworth became the governor after his uncle, Governor Benning Wentworth, resigned in 1766.

Simply put, England needed the largest pines they could find for the mighty Royal Navy. The massive white pines that King George coveted were standing 150 to 240 feet high in abundance in the northeastern part of the New World and were distinguished as the lightest and largest of all the wood used in the world to make masts. England's thirst to dominate the world's seas required the strongest and fastest ships they could build. With their forests depleted of proper mast-building trees, they were forced to find them elsewhere. Unfortunately, the desirable white pines were thriving on the lands owned by colonists like Ebenezer Mudgett.

Prior to the enforcement of the Crown's Pine Tree

Law, Ebenezer profited by sending his logs to Portsmouth in New Hampshire and Newburyport in Massachusetts to become masts for the hundreds of ships manufactured there yearly. Governor John Wentworth was obstructing Mudgett's successful business by enforcing the King's edict. Ebenezer was not the only person affected by the law. Every settler in the Northeast felt the hardship of relinquishing their timber to the Crown.

William Little's *The History of Weare, New Hampshire 1735-1888*, published by the town in 1888, served as a major reference for this book. In 1888 Little and his researchers interviewed the descendants of the early settlers and recorded many details of daily life in the 18th century. He captured some interesting barroom stories and jokes that I included in the language in which he wrote them. The chapter in the weighty tome dedicated to the Pine Tree Riot provided a skeleton of events leading to and including the infamous scene on April 14, 1772, and I was forced to speculate to fill in some of the details of what could have transpired. Also left to the imagination were any physical characteristics or personalities, except for Benjamin Whiting, the sheriff, who Little described as being hated by all, and William Dustin, described as being very skinny.

As is often the case, history repeats itself. We have seen in each century that resistance has often proved successful. Marches, sit-ins, boycotts, email and letter campaigns have fueled the fire of change in our lifetime. In 1772 the Weare men did not have the 21st-century tools to resist pacifically. One of the few options left to them to change the course of events was violence. With regard to the Pine Tree Riot, was it warranted? You be the judge.

The King's Broad Arrow

The sound of approaching horses made Ebenezer Mudgett's stomach drop. Ebenezer shaded his eyes against the glaring sun to confirm the identity of the riders nearing his home. As they drew closer, he knew that no introduction would be necessary. He knew exactly who they were. And the purpose of their visit. He had anticipated their arrival for a while. Still, he felt his muscles tense and his insides knot. Any remnant of a smile from the amusing story Abraham Johnson had been relating disappeared from his face.

In spite of the persistent, May black flies, Eb had been enjoying the kicking and bucking of the active foal born just two days ago. He removed his cap and grabbed at his ears where the pests were exchanging itchy welts for his blood. After giving his scalp a good scratching, Eb waved the cap vigorously around his head and quickly popped it back on, hoping to discourage other flies from landing on his gray-streaked hair. He shifted his position to lean on the fence with his arms resting on the top rail and changed his weight to his left leg. At forty-six years old, he found that his right hip needed to be assuaged every once in a while, especially since a recent fall from his stacked timber at Clement's sawmill. The mare, seemingly grateful to be outside in the warm spring air, was lazily munching on hay while emitting soft whinnies to remind her colt not to stray too far. Her tail and ears were in constant motion twitching the flies away. The foal's only defense was to run and kick. Ebenezer was about to head back to the house for the tin of lard and tar that helped to discourage the nasty flies when he noticed Abraham riding toward him carrying a sack on his horse.

Abraham Johnson was always a bit disheveled. His uncombed hair stuck out from all sides of his woolen cap rather than being neatly secured in a queue by a leather cord like most men. Even while serving in the French and Indian War, his colonel's admonition directed at his unkempt hair had little effect. His wife was equally remiss in ignoring the buttons that his round belly had popped off some time ago, and the one secured at the top of his vest only accentuated the bulge. In spite of his appearance, one could not help but return his trademark jovial smile.

"Mornin', friend! I suppose ye could use this sack of dried beans with all those children of yours. Even after this winter, we still have more than we can eat," Abraham offered.

"Are ye sure ye didn't want to show up without something to trade fer the ale ye'll be askin' fer? Ebenezer laughed. Eb immediately dismissed the mental list of work he had planned to do. He knew Abraham would be much more entertaining than liquor supply lists and splitting wood. Soon the two were stretched out, enjoying the sunshine, leaning up against the fence, and passing a jug between them. As they drank, Ebenezer became less sensitive to the flies and more intent on Abraham's gossip. Eb always enjoyed conversations with Abraham. His penchant for gossip invariably made Ebenezer laugh; however, the delivery was often more comical than the content. One of Eb's favorite topics was the on-going, good-natured bickering between the stocky, handsome twenty-year old Jotham Tuttle and the skinny, middle-aged William Dustin. William was well-liked, despite the fact that his wife had a reputation for being a witch, and they owned Rose, the only slave in Weare. Jotham enjoyed ribbing William, who feigned indignation but generally found the younger man's verbal jabs based on the truth.

"So, Jotham said to William yesterday," Abraham began trying to imitate Jotham, "*why would I steal yer axe! It wouldn't be hung right fer me! It doesn't fit me like this one!* And then Jotham picked up his own axe by the helve and showed William how well it balanced in his hand! "*Besides*, Jotham said to William, *Ye left yer axe in a tree overnight t'other day, and everybody knows that only brings bad luck, that's why ye can't find it!*" Ebenezer chuckled and Abraham was about to elaborate when the sound of the approaching riders curtailed the story.

The procession was taking its time; the horses' heads hung down in a relaxed manner, their ears twitched as the vexatious flies found an easy blood source. As they approached, the riders were shifting in their saddles and craning their necks to make a cursory assessment of the property. A few stately deciduous trees provided some shade on the sloping front lawn, but the wall of trees on the other side of a clearing behind the house drew the riders' attention. The interspersed oaks, birches, and maples hadn't fully leafed out, accentuating the majestic white pines.

For several years the settlers in Weare had been protected from the enforcement of the King's Pine Tree Law by the thick forests and challenging means of travel between Portsmouth, where the governor resided, and their homesteads. As the old Indian trails through the forests widened with increased travel, the governor's deputies were finding their ways to the remote villages and towns.

"Well, friend, it seems the governor's men have sniffed out yer trees." Abraham, also, had identified the nature of the visit.

The man leading the group addressed them. His diminutive stature and querulous voice would not have commanded the same attention without the advantage of his title. The man lifted his head and lowered his eyes to assume a measure of importance that his voice betrayed.

"I am *Deputy* John Sherburn. By order of the Crown we are here to carve the Royal broad arrow into your mast-worthy trees, sir," he stated, squaring his shoulders.

Ebenezer's inhibitions had loosened after consuming a good quantity of ale with Abraham. He struggled to stand, owing equal amounts of effort to his sore hip and from the ale he had consumed.

"The Crown!" Ebenezer responded. His deep voice did not have to be raised to emphasize his disgust. "May the Crown be damned! Tell the Crown . . ." Abraham threw out his arm, the back of his hand hitting his friend in the stomach. "Don't, Eb! Don't say another word!"

The deputy dismounted and with a wry smile, led his horse closer to the two men while the other riders proceeded around the house and beyond the clearing. Ebenezer noted the small man was struggling to remain calm. His girlish voice developed a slight tremor and cracked.

"Mr. Mudgett!" He cleared his throat and shifted his gaze from one man to the other. "This should be no surprise to ye, sir. Ye pay fer the license on yer trees, and we mark the ones over twelve inches in diameter as Governor Wentworth has instructed us. Do not protest, sir. It is the King's Pine Tree Law."

"Not protest! How can I not! I have put years into this land already. Though I object to payin' for the damned license, I shall do so. But I will not relinquish the trees standin' on the land that I bought with valid currency!" Meanwhile, Sherburn's stance reflected his authority: He stood erect with arms crossed. A triumphant smirk showed on his face.

Rattled by the deputy's air of superiority, Ebenezer inflated his chest like a sage grouse, catching Sherburn off-guard. The deputy had not encountered any difficulty from other settlers, barring some angry looks and muttering; he was unaccustomed to being challenged. Expecting a blow, the man quickly put up his arms and took a step backward.

"Now, Mr. Mudgett," his voice cracked again. Then lowering his voice, he said, "It will do ye no good to cause trouble. I have the broadsheet here that gives the governor, under orders from the King, the right to put the royal mark into the trees of a certain size. Ye may not like it, sir, but they do not belong to ye now."

"What does the King do for us in return? We have no say in Parliament; our governor is but a mere puppet! Where is the representation to deal with this sacrifice?"

"Leave it be, friend, leave it be," Abraham hissed under his breath, "ye can't argue with the Crown."

Ebenezer looked at his friend and bit his bottom lip. The strong ale he had shared with Abraham, coupled with the knowledge that his wife was not within earshot, had loosened Ebenezer's tongue. He had a lot to lose for even threatening to interfere with the order of the King. Instinctively, he turned to look toward the house. He did not see any anxious faces peering out the front windows. Miriam might be alerted by any more loud exchange. She certainly would be upset to hear him speaking harshly to the governor's deputy. He knew that his vociferous objections against the King would panic her, and her reaction would consternate the children for sure. The young ones would then run to the windows, or worse, come outside to witness their father disparaging an official of the King. He drew a deep breath. Whenever his sense of justice was challenged, Ebenezer could not let it be. He had to try now. In spite of his objections, he noted that the violation of his trees was beginning. The hacking of the royal symbol beyond the clearing seemingly took on an angry, cryptic conversation from one man's hatchet to another. He bit his lip harder.

The confrontation with John Sherburn ended with Ebenezer registering Abraham's fearful expression. The look on Abraham's face and the thought of Miriam and his family helped Mudgett resist expressing further recriminations.

With an exaggerated sweeping of his arm, Ebenezer's grand gesture pretended to welcome Sherburn to join his men in the defilement of his white pine trees. Sherburn snickered and mounted his horse. As he passed the men, the colt, who had been curious about the visitors, bucked, kicked, and scampered to his mother.

"I think we'll be seein' a lot more of these men 'round here," Abraham stated. Eb acknowledged the comment with a slight nod of his head and a long sigh that carried with it a defeated sounding, "Ayup." Abraham gave Eb two quick pats on his back and admitted he best be heading home. He, too, would be getting the unwelcome guests sometime shortly. Ebenezer watched his friend mount his horse and gave him a half-raised hand in farewell. He then turned to walk toward the house; his shoulders slumped in defeat. He would endeavor to be calm as he explained to his family what was transpiring on their property.

Ebenezer slowly walked up the slope to where his home stood. The two-story clapboarded house was built on a high point, and no doubt, Miriam was well aware of the activity going on in the back. Ebenezer stepped one foot on the front step and hesitated. With head down in thought, he silently pledged that he would do whatever he could to put an end to the Pine Tree Law and stop the confiscation of the white pine trees. He had no idea what, but he had to to do something.

Miriam was standing in the doorway holding the baby. She didn't have to verbalize her concern; her distressed look told him she knew what was happening behind their house. He lowered his head in disgust, and for the first time was aware of the itchy welt and congealed blood behind his right ear.

"They've come to take possession of our trees. I won't be able to sell any more decent-sized timber to the shipbuilders in Newburyport. Clement's sawmill will lose business as others are affected, and newcomers will have a harder time building their homes with the small pines. We all came here to make a decent living for our children. It seems like we will never get out from under England's control."

Miriam was not hearing anything she did not already know. "Husband, we are better off than most. You still have a profitable business selling spiritous liquors." Ebenezer gave her a half-hearted smile; she always had a way of diffusing a bad situation, but he knew she was just as worried as he was. At least her comment took the rough edges off his anger.

Ebenezer looked at his youngest child and wondered what kind of future he would have. Would the Crown have more demands by the time John is a young man going out on his own?

For the rest of the day and well after supper Ebenezer could not shake the growing animosity against the authority that was robbing what rightly belonged to him. He had tried to soothe his anger with an ample quantity of rum, but it only seemed to magnify his resentment. He was well-aware of Miriam's nervous, furtive looks indicating that she was worried about him.

When the evening chores occupied everyone, he slipped out of the house undetected by the housemaid, his children, or Miriam. Once outside, he walked with purpose to the woodshed, and opening the creaking door, he lifted the lantern above his head and spotted the hatchet.

Quimby's Inn

*E*benezer Mudgett was an integral member of the growing community. Friends came to rely on him for his decisiveness in handling situations and dispersing information. On his travels, he acquired gossip, general information, and political news that made him a welcome and valuable addition to any gathering. Tired settlers, worn out from clearing their land and fighting Mother Nature, crossed a tavern's threshold with a thirst for knowing what was happening outside the confines of their small, insular worlds as much as a thirst for a pint. Ebenezer, more often than not, was their only connection to the outside world.

On this brisk January day, he had braved the gusts of icy wind to walk the short distance to Quimby's Inn, the first inn in Weare, to check on Aaron Quimby's rum supply.

"Humph . . . Waya minute," Samuel said. Samuel Goodale had just arrived in Weare with a leather bag containing a few pounds and shillings and less chattel than most, basically an axe and a jug, both highly protected and cherished possessions in the wilderness. The last few days he had fashioned himself a temporary den to ward off the elements and critters, but he had designs to build a proper log cabin, fine enough to attract a hardy wife. Like many early settlers who came to Weare, Samuel was eager to engage with his neighbors; they would help him clear land and build his cabin, and eventually, he would reciprocate for the help. This brought him to Quimby's Inn to supply himself, sample the goods, and to share the air with other human beings.

Ebenezer studied Samuel and watched as the young man succumbed to the power of the warmed flip made with West India rum, dried pumpkin, apple skins, and bran. An almost imperceptible smile twitched at the corners of the older man's mouth.

"Are ye sayin' that we don't have a claim on our own trees? Pines that grow on our own land?" Samuel's head bobbed up, down, and around, accentuating some of his words like an owl triangulating on prey.

If the topic were anything else, Ebenezer would have enjoyed the scene more. Indeed, it was entertaining observing the flip master Samuel's speech, but the subject matter quickly wiped away any vestige of a smile Eb had. He noted from Samuel's expression that the young man had finally understood the severity of the conversation.

"I have plans for my big trees, and I'm not 'bout to

giv'em to *Georgie* on t'other side of the ocean. I don' care if he is our *King!*" He hesitated and then added while spilling some flip on his moose-hide trousers, "'Sides let him come *hisself.* See if he can rip 'em outta the ground! Ha!"

As is customary, conversation at Quimby's Inn began on an even keel but soon escalated into a loud phalanx of experts on any given topic. It was like a day starting with a soft wind that surged into a hurricane. On this cold, blustery day there were approximately eight men that stopped by to share and listen to stories—some true, some partially true, and some outrageous exaggerations. Consequently, the flip was starting to turn the conversation more voluble and severe.

Ebenezer sat quietly at the three-legged round cricket table in the corner. Daylight was short, and Aaron scurried around lighting the candles. The innkeeper had to avoid a lethargic man propped up on an elbow, stretched out on the wide-pine floor. The man was still wearing the leather apron that protected his moose-hide trousers when working in the woods. There were enough empty seats around small, round tables, but Eb surmised the man felt too confined to sit at one. An orange glow emanated from the fireplace. Soot from several years of roaring fires stained the ceiling. Cast-iron pots containing soup and beans hung on long iron arms suspended over the embers in the front while the big logs burned in the back. Next to the slate hearthstone were two large oak logs that would be a struggle to maneuver into the fiery cavity; a variety of iron tools hung nearby to help with the procedure. Enticing aromas wafted out of the pots, mixing with the smoke and rank smell of the man on the floor.

Eb was not eager to interject his thoughts on the matter of the pine trees, a subject that was having a significant impact on the tall, thin newcomer, Samuel. Even when heads turned in Ebenezer's direction and eyes begged for his commentary, which was usually forthcoming, he remained quiet. He sat with his left index finger over his top lip and his thumb tucked under his chin as if to silence his voice for fear his secret would slip out. The thumb of his right hand slid up and down the exterior of his pewter mug. The subject of the white pines was a disturbing and sensitive issue in the region, most of all to Ebenezer, especially since the night he went on his rampage and eradicated the royal marks, making the situation worse and leaving no doubt that the symbol had existed in the bark at one time. No one knew that the topic of the white pines was making his stomach knot. No one, perhaps, but Abraham. He admitted to Abraham that after Sherburn had left that May day, he foolishly hacked away the broad arrow marks. To exasperate the situation, his son, Moses, had helped him saw a few down. Ebenezer was ashamed when Abraham asked if he were joking.

"Samuel, I'm tellin' ye . . . That new Governor Wentworth is serious," Aaron signaled a large piece of paper with his elbow so as not to spill the freshly poured, steaming liquid. If Samuel knew how to read, he didn't show much interest in getting the details off the broadsheet.

The Weare patrons, seated on benches at the long table in the middle of the room, looked to Ebenezer again. He was the one that always did the informing, and then the others were the ones who filled in with their opinions. Ebenezer, ultimately unable to keep silent, reluctantly joined the conversation. "Look, Samuel, the thing is, he is goin' to come . . . Well, not exactly the governor himself, but he sends his men, his deputies of the woods. His Majesty has given the governor a title; it's on the broadsheet there . . ." He rose stiffly out of his chair, stretched his sore hip, and strode over to the wall. Tucking his chin down into his stock, he squinted, "Yes, here it is, Governor Wentworth is *Surveyor-of-the-King's-Woods*," he said, emphasizing the title as if it were a joke.

"That weasel Wentworth sent out his deputies to sniff 'round a while back, cuttin' foolish marks on our pines and demandin' we pay fer a license on the rest of 'em. They ain't friendly 'bout it either," said Timothy Worthley, futilely swiping away the strands of hair that always managed to escape from his leather tie-back.

Timothy's brother, Jonathan, added, "Samuel, ye have ta get tha license before clearin' or buildin' anything. Ye can be arrested an' fined if ye don't." As was often the case, Jonathan looked to Timothy for confirmation. Timothy nodded, releasing another strand from his plait.

"Thas right, don' even start yer pole and bark roof or top out the cobbles and clay on yer chiminey!" The rum had fattened Jotham Tuttle's tongue. "I canna unnerstan' takin' a man's property righ' out from unner 'im." Strapping young Jotham was very familiar with the Pine Tree Law and the fine for sawing one of the marked trees down. He and his father had felled two marked pines, and before they could plank and hide them, John Sherburn had made an appearance. They could have been jailed if they had not come up with the fine. "Wentworth's men'll be makin' their way here again to carve the King's claim in yer trees with three slashes; they call it the King's Broad Arrow. Looks more like a crow's foot to me!"

Ebenezer shut himself off again from the conversation. His left hand rose to his mouth with the index finger and thumb back in place. He needed to bury the unpleasant memories bubbling to the surface, especially while in the company of others. Instead, he focused on his upcoming trip to Salem and made mental notes of the supplies he would need.

William Dustin had just pulled out the chair across from Ebenezer and said, while easing his small frame down, "Ebenezer, ye had pointed out many times to anybody who'd listen that John Wentworth's stubbornness regardin' the Pine Tree Law has reached Weare. Sooner than later, we are *all* goin' to feel the measure of his authority." He slapped the table for emphasis. "Governor Wentworth's greed for his majesty is far-reachin'; he wants to attract the King's attention by enforcin' the despicable law. He feels if a few coins find their way into his pockets, so be it. We all know he hopes to find violations." The men all nodded in unison and mumbled unintelligible words of agreement. William's bony fingers combed through his brown, wavy beard, a habit he had when he said something he perceived to be important.

"Wentworth's greedy and if he catches ya, hopes ye'll pay a large sum to settle. Or he can auction off the logs an' fine ya ta boot," offered Caleb Atwood, a rosy-cheeked man in the corner. *Why doesn't Caleb change the subject by tellin' one of his funny stories*, Ebenezer thought. Catching Caleb in a serious mood was rare.

"I didn't much care for his uncle, tha' Guv'ner *Benning* Wentworth," Jotham added. "But at least he didn't enforce the law like his slimy-nosed nephew's doin'. 'Til recently no one bothered with us in the woods here."

Caleb stood up to make a point but needed to steady himself with the table. Leaning on it, he said, "We need our pines, goddammit! How can we make planks to build our houses? We have ta build barns, meetin' houses . . . an' even bridges! It just is not right for the King to claim *our* trees on *our* lands for hisself, for *England*!"

Like many settlers in New Hampshire, the Stamp Act was of little concern to the Weare families, but the Pine Tree Law was more than a disturbance; it was like a noose cutting into their livelihoods and strangling their opportunities for a foothold in the community. The Stamp Act required colonists to pay a tax on every piece of printed paper they used, even playing cards. Many of the Weare residents could go weeks or months without laying a hand on a printed page and a few more probably never touched one. The Pine Tree Law directly affected all families because they were establishing a town and needed the large, tall pines to do it.

"What's he doin' with all the trees?" Samuel cocked his head to the side. His eyebrows pushed together in a frown.

Sighing deeply, Ebenezer stated, "It takes a lot of trees to build one ship, Samuel. England has used up their good wood. They need ours."

The Worthley brothers were nodding in unison as if they had two bodies and one head. With his fingers, Timothy combed the escaped lock of hair away from his eyes again and shared, "I hear Wentworth hadn't bothered with our towns before 'cause it hurt his tender arse ridin' this far from Portsmouth. He's gotten a bit greedy . . . Or his arse has toughened." He leaned back in his chair, surveyed the room for validation of his joke and grinned when the rest of the men rewarded him with a chuckle.

"If he does come, he'll set his tender backside in a carriage. But I bet our trail will give him a rough ride." Then Ebenezer added more seriously, "No, we haven't been seein' him much. It's his deputies that make the journey." Then he mumbled, "Especially that John

Sherburn."

"That runt Sherburn's got a funny high voice," said Abraham Johnson, who had turned to address Ebenezer. "Ye heard 'im, Eb. He came to yer place last May, remember?" Abraham's mouth stretched into a smile, revealing an eager face waiting for a good story to unravel.

Ebenezer immediately regretted that he had brought up John Sherburn's name and fell silent. Without thinking, he had opened a new avenue in the conversation that the bibulous man was encouraging Ebenezer to take. Abraham was known to throw out a seed for another to grow. To be sure, Eb despised the little emissary of the governor as much for marking the trees as for the gleefulness with which he performed his duty. Eb was just determined not to allow them to drag him into relating the embarrassing situation that occurred *after* Sherburn had left. He made a subtle inclination of his head in agreement. Hopefully, Abraham wouldn't pressure him to relate his story.

"Tha' John Sherburn is like an annoyin' mosquito whinin' 'round yer head," piped up Jotham.

"The sheriff is the one ye all should fear!" Caleb blurted out, louder than he expected. "If a man was headin' for a scuffle, Sheriff Benjamin Whiting is *not* the man to confront." The general scuttlebutt was that in addition to being pompous and relying on his prestigious position for leverage, Whiting was also irascible, dispersing acrimony wherever he went.

"If Sherburn is a mosquito, then Whiting is a

hornet. He can sting, and he has the full blessin' of the guv'nor to support him. No, Benjamin Whiting is *not* to be agitated," Jonathan said, eyeing Timothy to validate his point. His brother nodded.

"Ayup, twelve inches in diameter gets yer tree that blasted King's mark," growled William, bobbing his head and stroking his beard.

Jotham laughed out loud. "William! You spend more time thinkin' on what was said ten minutes ago than focusin' on the new conversation! Yer always 'bout ten minutes behind!"

William raised his tankard in Jotham's direction and replied, "Well, young friend, I'm still followin' the general flow of it."

The Journey's Preparation

Aaron was starting to pour some more flip into Samuel's glass. The young man raised his hand and waved it in a gesture indicating he had had enough. His hand fell back on the rough-hewn table. He needed to process what he had heard.

"No more, Mr. Quimby. I need ta go. Soon I'll be seein' the sun settin' behind the hills." His thickening tongue was laboring to pronounce certain words. He pulled out a few coins from the leather pouch tucked in his trousers.

"I respect a man who knows his limits!" Aaron said, clapping Samuel on his back and accepting payment.

"Don't chop down anythin,' Samuel. Wait for the 'spection. They are bound ta be here pokin' 'round," warned Caleb. "In the meantime, we're fixin' ta go to Salem for some barterin'. Yer welcome to join us, and it'll keep ye busy til they locate yer land. I'll have some room on my pung fer yer goods if ye want ta go."

"We're meetin' on the south road near Clement's Mill soon as the sun is up," William said.

"I suppose I could trade sumthin' fer my beaver skins," Samuel said with a smile, raised one arm in a half-hearted farewell, and stumbled out the door.

Suddenly, the conversation took on a life of its own. The men, fortified with the flip, were considerably more brazen.

"I say we tar 'n feather Wentworth 'n Sherburn!"

"Send 'em bound and gagged up ta Quebec and let the French at 'em!"

"Tie 'em naked to a tree and dump molasses on their heads!"

Ebenezer sensed it was prudent to retreat from the exchange and wait for the excess of rum to perform its final function: making utterances so incomprehensible that they were nearly impossible to understand, slowing the discussion to a trickle, then a halt. Feeling satisfied that they had indeed provided sound solutions to their shared predicament, the spirit-sodden bodies exited one by one, laughing and stumbling, after either signing a note to forestall payment or leaving some previously agreed-upon commodity for barter.

The flip seemed to turn bitter in Ebenezer's mouth. He had not divulged that he ignored the despicable law. He stared at the remains of the flip and recalled the night after Sherburn and his men left. Speaking seditiously against the monarch, he stumbled out to his big pines and obliterated the broad arrows. In between hackings, he shouted invectives to each tree, specifying what the majesty could do with his law. Afterward, he was thoroughly exhausted. His balance was in jeopardy. He bent over to catch his breath and leaned on his axe for support. He surveyed the damage and, mopping his brow, became slightly ashamed of his effrontery. Nevertheless, he regained his breath and composure and proceeded to whack the broad arrow sign into smaller trees, as if that would rectify the contravention. He kept quiet about his culpable logs, now piled high at the mill, the timber due to be planked shortly. He twirled the remains of his flip, now cooled, and stared into his mug. His pines presently stacked at Clement's sawmill were a good size, well over the twelve-inch diameter coveted by King George—and they all had distinctive scars at the same height.

He tried to push the thought to the recesses of his brain, hoping that time would be in his favor. Either Wentworth or Sherburn would be checking for offending trees at the sawmills; the men's arrival would never be announced. He had a sick feeling it was imminent. He should go to the mill and urge the log-cutters to get his timber milled posthaste; however, he had to keep the business afloat. To accomplish this, he had persuaded his friends to ready their oxen the following day for a journey to Salem. Buying the barrels of rum would help keep his business running steadily and his family fed. In addition to Quimby's, he knew of at least eight inns or taverns along the route that would be close to running low, mainly due to the general commiseration from the governor's enforcement of the Pine Tree Law. His pung couldn't carry all his customers' rum at one time as well as the supplies his family would require, therefore, he would be doing another trip or two before spring.

Ebenezer took a mental inventory of his current supply of spirits. The cider he had recently made from the apples on his land was stored in the cellar hole and would last through February, another month, but not much longer. Upon his return, he'd teach his eldest son, Moses, the simple process of making the hard cider: allowing it to freeze and then separating the ice from the alcohol. There was always a greater demand for it over the plain cider by virtue of its desired effect. He also had a good supply of his own ale; however, the real attraction was the West Indies rum. It was common for a man to consume four to five gallons of hard liquor each year, rum being the preferred choice, even though the tax was high. The only way to supply his rapacious customers was to make several arduous journeys a year to a distillery in Salem, Massachusetts. Each trip usually required an absence of up to two weeks, during which Miriam would have to parcel out his chores to their oldest male children, Moses, eighteen, and Ezra, twelve.

The Weare farmers enjoyed making the trip to the market a community affair. Their ox teams joined five or six others that needed to do their trading in the coastal towns. Sometimes they would go south into Newburyport, sometimes east to Portsmouth. They bartered their goods for what they could not grow or make at home. Their favorite destination was Salem, where they had a greater variety of household items. Each farmer loaded his surplus products onto his pung, a box-like sled that made winter traveling easier. If he didn't have a full load, he was obliged to take some of a neighbor. Among the animal skins, whole frozen hogs, butter, cheese, poultry, grains, wool, yarn, flax, dried apples, and other farm products packed onto the sled was a big tub of frozen bean porridge. A hatchet accompanied it to break the gruel into chunks to heat up in the taverns they frequented. They also had a good supply of baked oatmeal bannocks and roasted meat to eat while on the road. It wasn't uncommon for the men to supplement their meals by grinding corn into a powder and mixing it with water to drink.

Rarely did they need to buy food en route. The taverns and inns along the way accepted, and in most cases preferred, that their clientele bring their own provisions. There was more money to make in serving the hot toddies and ales. The innkeepers had hay and water for the travelers' cattle, but the farmers always included several bushels of oats and corn to supplement their animals' feed.

Ebenezer enjoyed the camaraderie on these trips; it wasn't hard to convince Jotham, William, and Caleb to go, and Samuel had accepted Caleb's invitation. Timothy Worthley and his brother, Jonathan, normally accompanied them on the Salem ventures, but Timothy's wife had taken sick and Jonathan had not chopped enough wood to last for a two-week absence. Abraham had to decline also, but between Jotham and

William, they would be able to make enough room on their pungs to take some of their friends' goods to barter. To keep rum flowing in Weare and the neighboring towns and villages, Ebenezer would also have to make one or two trips on his own, but they weren't nearly as much fun.

Most likely, the unpredictable weather would not be their ally during the entire two-week journey; however, he was hopeful for tolerable conditions. You had to be resilient in this environment if you were dependent on Mother Nature; she could be undeniably beautiful and tender like a mother with a newborn babe, or violent and tempestuous like an enraged shrew. You had to accept the dual personality and acknowledge that the appearance of one would be temporary, with the other soon to follow.

Even so, only a fool would attempt the journey during certain seasons. In the spring, the rain and subsequent mud rendered the road impossible, sucking and grabbing at anybody or anything that dared to pass over it. It was as though angry trolls lived under the sludge—clutching at the hooves and heels of man and beast. Small black flies and mosquitoes hatched in abundance in the spring, making the journey more difficult. The summer months had their own miseries: The sun's rays bore mercilessly right through a man, causing rivulets of sweat to trickle down from his forehead, his chest, and back, and drying the tongue until it was like a flap of parchment. After a heavy rain in the summer, a blistering hot sun could bake the mud, making the ruts hard as dried clay. A man would then have to navigate as best he could to avoid the deep trenches. To venture out in the fall was certainly preferable to spring or summer, but the best time to travel was after the snow fell, and there were several inches of a nicely laid carpet to make the pungs slide all the way to Salem. The trick was to go before the snow got knee-deep and to try not to get caught in a thaw.

"Miriam, come to bed. I need yer warmth!" he joked. The candlelight was not bright enough to record her features, but he instinctively knew she was smiling.

"Just a minute, husband. I need to finish combing my hair. I think the baby's sticky fingers got sumthin' in there." He loved to watch her comb out the luxurious brown hair that she kept hidden under a cap by day. He relished the privilege of watching it spill out and tumble down her back, an intimacy unknown to bachelors like Samuel.

"I was gettin' a bit uneasy at Quimby's. With the spirits loosenin' their tongues, the men forgot that a Tory could have been among them. Speakin' ill of the King's supporters would be a transgression with a penalty if overheard by the wrong person. Tis dangerous to be right when the King is wrong. I guess I have ole Governor Wentworth to thank for the increase in business. More men are needin' to share their concern with a pint of somethin'. This newly enforced Pine

Tree Law is going be hard on everyone, Miriam, even us." He paused and held up the quilt for her to join him. "We need the pine boards to add another section to the house. Also, the barn could use two extra stalls."

She snuggled close to him. He put his arm around her. She sighed contentedly as she wiggled into his body to take advantage of the warmth and the feel of his strong arm.

"I've gone through more rum than usual, and I fear I need ta get movin' down to Salem before we get piled high with more snow. Ye'll be good with that?"

"I'll make my list . . . and get some things ready for barterin'." He was always aware of the resignation in her voice whenever he proposed making the journey.

"Don't ferget the mittens I just finished. I knitted them double, should keep yer hands warmer than the other pair ye had." He knew better than to turn over and fall asleep; he could tell by the increased speed in her voice that she was just getting started with her advice and admonitions.

"Oh, and don't ferget the calicoes this time, lord knows little Miriam will need a new summer dress, the way she's sproutin'. I need a good bowl for bread makin' 'cause Moses dropped my other. Don't ferget to take the yarn and linen cloth . . ."

"Don't forget the molasses mother needs and my hair ribbons!" Pretty fourteen-year old Sarah yelled, appearing in the doorway.

"You promised me a huntin' knife the last trip!" Ezra said, pushing Sarah aside.

Suddenly little Miriam poked her head between them and laughed, "The sugared almonds, father, the sugared almonds!"

"I know, dear hearts, I have it all written here," he tapped his temple.

The Farewell

It was the kind of crisp, frosty morning in late January that energized Ebenezer. He and Miriam had risen early. Trying not to wake the baby, Miriam was whispering all the last-minute advice and reminders she had swirling around in her head before Ebenezer's departure.

"I need ta get my team set now." He put on his thick overcoat followed by his blue frock coat and wrapped a muffler tightly around his neck, being sure to cover his nose and ears. After he adjusted his wolf-skin hat, he put on the mittens, turned to face her, and raised his hands up to show his appreciation; they would be a blessing on the trail.

He held his lantern high to cast some light on the path. The thin layer of freshly fallen snow glittered as the snow crystals reflected the light. The packed snow underneath crunched and squeaked under his cowhide boots. Nip and Tuck turned in his direction and greeted him with small clouds of steam rising from their nostrils. He yoked the oxen, hitched them to the pung and filled the sled box with the barter trade for the Salem market. He started with the thirty-gallon barrels for the rum he would be buying and then filled the rest of his products inside the casks. Finally, he hoisted the tub of frozen bean porridge onto the back.

He bounded into the house to find Miriam, who was tending to the crying baby and trying to mediate the first of the day's disagreements among the rest of the children. He opened his mouth in feigned surprise.

"My, my, my. Have you sweet children risen early to wish your dear father a safe trip? Or," he hesitated, "are ye here to make more special requests? Hmmm?" He playfully grabbed the necks of the two nearest children, ten-year old Achsah and seven-year old William, and shook them. "Am I right, you naughty ones?"

Five-year old Miriam and her younger brother Jesse started jumping up and down, clapping their hands together and squealing with joy. "Both, Papa, both!"

He knew that Salem was a mysterious, exciting place to them, and they would be anxiously waiting for his pung to return, loaded to the hilt with wonderful surprises. His reward for the arduous journey was always the unbridled joy that greeted him after the long trip.

The loudly uttered solicitations made John wail even louder. The housemaid, Claire, picked the baby up and tried to soothe him by holding him close and whispering in his ear. It was no use; he wanted what only his mother could provide.

"Mercy! Can I leave from under this roof just once without all this caterwauling?" Eb said with a hint of a smile.

"Oh, Ebenezer! You aren't foolin' me!" Miriam shouted over the din, nursing John as she walked. "Your mood is very gay with the prospect of a journey. I suspect, dear husband, you relish the escape from a household of eight children!" Ebenezer returned her ribbing with a smile. He knew she also yearned for an escape every once in a while, but her days of accompanying him were well in the past.

Departing always seemed a little awkward; he wondered if she felt a bit abandoned, even though she would never say it. Sandwiched between timid three-year-old Jesse and seven-year-old William, she concentrated her gaze on her husband until he met her eyes. Both were silently speaking the language that years of a happy marriage had taught them. Only then did she hold out the large sack of provisions that she had hurriedly gathered: bannocks, hunks of roasted meat, cheese, and apples. He grasped the neck of the sack, but Miriam held onto it and continued staring into his eyes. She released the rations only when he gave her a nod and grateful smile. He hoped he was able to conceal his impatience to get underway. She was right, he was looking forward to the journey, but there was also a nagging reminder that warned him to return quickly to the sawmill to hide the contraband.

The only one not begging for something was

Achsah. She always tended to melt into the group, never voicing her thoughts, but always entertained by the demonstrations and chaos her brothers and sisters produced. She was the child most overlooked, the well-greased wheel that didn't demand attention. She stood in the background, smiling.

Miriam's silence would only serve to reinforce her envy, so she did her best to be heard over the clamor, "You know that Ezra and Moses will be more than capable of handling the outside chores and helping with the heavy work. Sarah, Achsah, Miriam, and William will do my bidding inside as usual. I suppose the others will help or hinder, according to their ages. No need to worry 'bout us, husband."

After kissing his wife and children goodbye, and with his brood clinging to him, he stumbled outside against the winter air and biting wind. Even among the chattering voices, loud sniffling, and jostling for coveted positions nearest their father, Eb was able to stop and close his eyes for a brief second or two. He inhaled deeply before another sudden, fierce blast of air sent icy needles jabbing his unprotected cheeks. The power of the stinging air produced querulous cries from the young children, except Jesse, who found some comfort burying himself in his mother's skirts. The others quickly abandoned their departing father to run back into the house and, like little chicks seeking the warmth of their mother, wiggle and nestle into the choicest spots near the fireplace.

"Watch that ye don't spill out the barrels," Miriam

said, hunching her shoulders to keep the wind from finding an entrance to her back. Eb knew she said it as though it were a charm against such a mishap, not from lack of confidence.

"Stop yer frettin', wife, I'll be home before ye know it." He cupped her chin and cheek tenderly and stared intently into her blue eyes. When had the deep azure dulled? When had they lost the sparkle that attracted him to the youthful, spirited girl? At least the cold air had brought back the rosiness in her cheeks. Earlier, one of the children had wrenched off her cap, allowing the sun to accentuate the golden highlights mixed with a few silver threads in her brown hair. She was still a handsome woman.

Eb gave her a peck on her cheek, and with a slight nod in her direction, he quickened his steps toward the barn where his restless beasts were anxiously waiting for the journey. Right now, he had to focus his attention on meeting the rest of the caravan and then getting to Reeds Ferry Landing, an important access site to the Merrimack River. They would cross on the ferry, conditions permitting, before heading to Salem.

The Journey Begins

The sun was slowly rising in the east and over the white pines mingled with naked oaks, birches, and maples. Occasional shafts of sunlight lit up the green velvet moss and lichen peeking out from patches of snow on the granite rocks. Soon the welcome sphere would shed a little warmth, but a lot of his journey would be shaded and cold. Many more years would be necessary to remove the massive old pines and other trees near the path to allow the sun's rays to warm the entire route. To keep the blood flowing between tavern stops, he and his friends would have to trot periodically behind their pungs.

Ebenezer snapped the goad and shouted, "Move on!" The steers responded by leaning, heads down, and pushing their lumbering bodies forward. The pung creaked a little; the sled blades dug into the snow until the momentum caused them to slide nicely.

He was the last to arrive at the arranged meeting area near the sawmill. Caleb was always the anxious one, invariably the first one there. Ebenezer attributed this to the fact that Caleb had been a soldier in the French and Indian War. The cold air made his plump cheeks look more like ripe McIntosh apples. Standing next to him was Samuel; his hat, knitted too large for his head, was almost covering his eyes. He pulled it up and greeted Eb with a broad smile.

"Mornin'! We thought you'd slept late!" joked William walking next to Samuel. "Looks like a beauty of a day. We can make good time if the trail is entirely passable." William's optimism was always qualified with an "if."

"Did ye manage to fit all of the Worthleys' and Abraham's goods between ye both? I might have a little room to help out on my pung," Ebenezer said.

The men walked over to Ebenezer's pung, piled much higher than any of theirs, and laughed.

"Could be ye have some room fer a flint or oil stone but nothin' more!" Caleb joked. Ebenezer always enjoyed having him on these journeys. Caleb was comical enough to squeeze a smile out of a statue.

Eb saw Jotham making adjustments on his pung and said, "Ye got yer Jotham Beans there?" His family was famous for making the best beans in Weare, and everybody referred to them as Jotham Beans. Jotham was always a good companion on these trips; he was good-natured but also robust enough to move substantial obstacles out of the trail. Furthermore, his frequent teasing of William was always entertaining.

"No Jotham Beans, no journey!" he laughed.

"That's right. We gotta have some music along the way!" Samuel turned around to see if his joke was understood. The men laughed, and then William acknowledged the joke with a loud release of his own. Jotham and Samuel laughed the loudest.

"Aw, William always likes to compete with the cattle!" Jotham laughed, "and he usually wins!"

Ebenezer chuckled with the others but knew if he didn't change the subject, there would invariably be more jokes about bodily functions. "Last time I went to Salem most of the trail was wide enough so the branches didn't hit the sides of my pung."

The original road was just an Indian path that he and other colonists had had a hand in widening with each trip. A jumper, or horse-barrow, encountered no real problems getting through, but the men required something a bit wider to accommodate their rigs. Like all travelers, their axes would be their constant companions, helping to extricate the unwelcome branches that prevented their progress on the smaller trails.

It would be into the next century before the entire route was broad enough to accommodate comfortably two passing wagons. The trail widened considerably when they joined the logging road in Goffstown. Transporting the mammoth pine logs destined for sailing ships was an engineering feat. The future mast would be rigged upon two giant pairs of wheels, each nine feet in diameter, with sixteen and sometimes as many as forty yokes of oxen pulling in front. On each side, two additional teams strained and pulled. It didn't take much hauling to carve out a decent-sized road. The road would eventually be known as Mast Road to remind further generations of the Crown's avarice.

"If we're lucky, we won't run into any northbound teams in the heavily wooded sections, Samuel," William said. "That's when it gets tricky!"

If such an unfortunate situation occurred, it often resulted in a test of wills as to which team or teams would be forced to retreat to the nearest passable area. The loathsome process involved unhitching the oxen and managing to turn the sled around, re-hitching them, only to repeat the process further down the road. Fights frequently broke out; stubborn men thrown together in this combative situation delayed them considerably. The unofficial signal to accede was first blood drawn. Nevertheless, put one or more tenacious, rum-filled blokes in the mix, and it could take a lot longer to resolve.

"It's kinda like that game the children play with music and chairs," William continued. "Ye want to encourage yer teams to go at a faster pace along the narrow paths, hoping to reach a safe spot to pass in case someone is comin' from the other way. But we don't have the music!"

"You want ta lead this time, Eb? My team's still a bit fresh, and they'll need ta follow a seasoned one,"

Jotham said. "I'll hang back in the rear."

Ebenezer steered Nip and Tuck with his voice commands, gee to go right and haw to go left, and used the goad as a follow-up until he positioned them in the front of the three other pungs; and so the long journey began. Any conversation between the five men would have to rise above the sounds of multiple hooves digging into the packed snow, the beasts' grunts and snorts, and the communication between oxen and drivers. Soon the men fell into a comfortable cadence and were enveloped in their own thoughts.

As was often the case on one of these journeys, Eb would feel the immediate, preternatural release from familiar pressures, as if he had suddenly sprouted wings and was soaring through the air. He loved his wife and children dearly; however, being on the road without their tentacles wrapped tightly around his mind and body gave him precious time and space to drift off into his own thoughts. He and Miriam had little opportunity for meaningful conversations or at least were never able to finish their discussions. It seemed that whenever they were afforded a few moments together, apart from their daily chores, an altercation with or between their offspring dominated the precious time. With the older children, it was like walking through the woods and trying not to set off a dozen invisible snares. The younger ones battled among themselves over any number of trivial causes. He thought of Miriam's look that could shrivel his insides whenever he made excuses for them—and smiled. He admitted to himself that he sometimes enjoyed taking the children's side, just to vex her a little.

Usually, as the trip lengthened, he forgot about the little quarrels and daily commotion in his home. His mind would begin to drift and conjure up an image of one of the children. This time it started with the sweet expression of Achsah, and then it was followed by the memory of an unselfish gesture by her younger brother William. The small acts of kindness, the generosity of spirit, and the sounds of the uncontrollable, infectious giggles that bounced off the walls of their house flooded his mind. He inhaled a chestful of air as he thought about Moses developing into a strong young man. He was able to split a log on the first try much better than last year! The two of them would accomplish a lot more now. Soon Ezra would join them. Ebenezer reflected that as he grew older and inexorably weaker, his boys, men, would be his muscle. But then, he thought miserably, they would move out and build homesteads of their own.

Snowflakes were beginning to fall a little more seriously. He had no way of knowing if this was the start of a significant snowfall or just a brief display of beauty. They melted directly upon landing; it was a good sign that he didn't have to brush them off yet. He put his head back, opened his mouth, and let them fall onto his tongue like he did when he was a boy. He smiled, enjoying the tiny prickles on his cheeks. The clouds hadn't completely covered the sky, allowing the sun to peek out occasionally to encourage the flakes to sparkle and shine as they drifted down. Suddenly, the wind picked up and whirled the snowflakes around; Nip and Tuck seemed impervious to the display but lowered their heads and trudged onward.

Ebenezer began to open and close his hands to get the blood circulating in his frozen fingers. It wasn't working. His hip and backside started to ache. He took his goad, got down, and jogged behind his pung. He flicked the goad twice to let the beasts know to keep moving. He pumped his arms and raised his fists chin-high, as if in a race, but his lower body was moving at a slower pace. He could barely feel his numb toes strike the packed snow. He turned around and noticed the other men were jogging as well. He knew there was a tavern not too far ahead. Soon they would be positioning themselves in front of the hearth and benefiting from the glorious warmth.

A traveler did not have to go more than about eight miles before he encountered a tavern; they were popping up regularly like dandelions in the spring throughout the rough thoroughfares of New England. After securing a license, a man needing some income could hang a shingle outside, fashion a table and chairs, and claim his home a business. Travelers like Ebenezer would need strong liquid and warmth to defrost useless hands and frozen toes; their teams would require water and rest along the route. From a business standpoint, Ebenezer needed to connect with the tavern-keepers, his customers, and see to getting orders that he would fill on his way back from Salem. The men always enjoyed the conversation and the good-natured ribbing exchanged with those they counted as friends en route to Massachusetts.

Nip and Tuck seemed to be moving well in their hypnotic trance, their heads swinging slightly in unison. He hardly had to use the goad. *These beasts of burden may not be the smartest of God's creatures,* he thought, *but they have enough sense to know when I will not spare the whip.* He was silently congratulating himself for having bought them as a pair, for they performed much better yoked together than apart. His thoughts were interrupted by a man shouting commands to his horse.

He peered around his pung and over the heads of his steers to see a horse-drawn sled fast approaching. The slippery conditions did not warrant such speed, he judged. The man was putting himself and his horse in jeopardy.

Mudgett swiftly surveyed the immediate area and saw that the narrow tree-lined path would be impossible to accommodate both north- and southbound travelers. The driver of the oncoming sled would have to find an area for the four teams to pass him, but the man in question was not slowing down and was approaching the bewildered Ebenezer shouting loudly, "Get outta tha way!"

The man yanked the reins and jerked his horse to a halt. He glared at Ebenezer. While keeping a secure hold on his steers, Mudgett shrugged his shoulders and tilted his head in a gesture indicating there was nothing he could do.

"Sir, ye can not possibly think that we would be able to turn 'round or back up easier and faster than you!" Ebenezer said.

"I need ta hurry!" the man said peremptorily. "I have urgent business!" The skin covering the prominent cheekbones was taut and rapidly turning a bright red as though he had two cherries on either side of his face. His hair was pulled back and secured with a ribbon that bobbed in time with the anxious prancing of his snorting horse who, it seems, had sensed his master's agitation. The man's ears were as red as his cheeks, making Eb wonder what urgency had caused the rider to leave without a hat.

"What do ye think we can do here, sir? We are unable to move to the side and there are four of us and only one of you," Ebenezer stated matter of factly. He was dumbfounded that this man, blocking the forward movement of the teams, would be such a numbskull as to think they could obey his outlandish demand. The two glared at each other. The other man clenched his teeth in exasperation. Finally, concluding that there really was nothing else he could do, the man pursed his lips, grunted, and exhaling a small, white cloud, angrily unhitched his horse. The men secured their oxen and helped him back his sled up to a wider area on the trail where he re-hitched his horse and waited. He did not acknowledge their help.

"Well then, get a move on!" he shouted to the Weare group. "You're holdin' up my official business!"

Eb was inclined to let Nip and Tuck take their time. He was annoyed by the absurdity of the fellow, but he snapped the goad and commanded the beasts onward at a good clip. The others, surprised by the rider's attitude, followed at the same speed. Eb smiled begrudgingly and nodded to the man as he passed; however, he was rewarded with a scowl that he suspected greeted each driver. Suddenly he heard a shout behind him.

"Hey! Goddamn it!" It was Jotham. Ebenezer joined William, Caleb, and Samuel to the rear where they found Jotham trying to salvage his famous beans.

"That bloody cockchafer!" He punched the air with his fist as the horse and driver were rapidly disappearing down the trail. "He had a stick and tipped my pot over!"

Jotham had removed his mittens and was scooping the cleanest of the frozen chunks of brown beans back into the pot. Samuel picked up a clump from the ground and examined it. He was brushing off the snow and dirt while the others tried to appease Jotham.

"They'll be fine ta eat still, and I have plenty of food, we won't starve," Ebenezer reassured him. They knew it wasn't the loss of the food that bothered Jotham.

"I saw the symbol of the Crown sewn onto his cloak," Caleb said.

"That was Sheriff Ben Whiting's deputy, John

Quigley. He was just appointed by the sheriff and maybe feels he has to be as offensive and derisive as his boss," William said, stroking his beard.

"The Goat's Head Tavern is just around the bend. I can almost smell the hot flip. We'll get a mug and put this situation to rest, Jotham," Caleb added, giving him a hearty slap on the back.

Mulling over the incident in his head, Ebenezer agreed that the best remedy to forget the entire nonsense was to get to the tavern. The pleasant, pungent smell of burning wood signaled their proximity. The prospect of the rum warming him up combined with seeing the owner, his good friend Daniel, helped to mitigate the recent nonsense.

The Goat's Head, a well-established, two-story clapboarded tavern with four sixteen-paned windows on either side of the oak door came into clear view. Tuck snorted and quickened his pace. Nip didn't have to be pulled; he too smelled the hay piled high in the barn. The goad would not be necessary to move them faster. The image of a nice warm fire brought a smile to Ebenezer's wind-abused face.

An Unfortunate Encounter

Ebenezer had just secured the oxen and was the last to leave the Goat's Head barn. He was pleased with himself that he had gotten this far without too many frustrating incidents. Of course, there was Quigley's aberrant attitude, but he was determined to put the incident out of his mind. Not counting that, the journey was going better than expected: The weather had been cold but invigorating, and they only had to chop a few felled branches from the trail to allow passage.

It was at this moment in his thoughts when he spotted *him*; he was standing in front of the tavern and was the focal point of four other men in a semi-circle facing him. They were laughing and enjoying the jocularity of his amusing story. Ebenezer had been drawn to the voice rising and floating to him like a bad smell. He began to feel in his stomach what his brain was registering. The high-pitched, nasally voice invoked a bad memory.

John Sherburn, noticeably pleased with himself, paused to take a breath. He had captivated his followers. He twisted partly around to see if the man approaching would be duly impressed. He turned back opened-mouthed to begin speaking to his friends again, then stopped. Mouth still agape, he whipped his head back again.

The deputy's smile slowly evaporated. It appeared that Sherburn also had a memory redolent of an unfortunate situation, a situation in which he struggled to achieve the upper hand. Ebenezer Mudgett was the one who had given him the most resistance he'd faced since he became the governor's deputy of the woods.

Taking leave of his audience, still chuckling over his tale, John Sherburn ambled over to the vulnerable newcomer with the stride of a man aware of his authority and confident he had the support of his friends.

"I know ye sir. Do I not?" It was more of a statement than an inquiry, but still requiring a response. Ebenezer decided to play the innocent.

"I don't believe so." Ebenezer, trying to be phlegmatic, walked past him. Sherburn took a side step to block his path. Ebenezer adjusted his action . . . But not enough. Being much shorter than Ebenezer, John's shoulder bumped against Mudgett's upper arm. The message his shoulder delivered was as clear as if he had spoken.

"I wish ta differ, sir."

Sherburn's group stopped laughing. They adjusted

their stances to hear the conversation better.

"Yer rantin' left a mark on me as deep as the ones we put into yer pines, the mast-worthy pines. Surely . . . ye could not forget the unfortunate way ye behaved?" His right hand found a resting place on his hip. His left arm hung awkwardly by his side. He decided to straighten his hat instead.

Mudgett stopped and turned. A sudden gust of wind lifted up newly fallen snowflakes that swirled and glittered in a miniature helix. He stared at the pugnacious man adjusting his tricorn and noted it was too large for his head. Ebenezer realized the deputy had backed him into a corner. He tried a new tactic.

"P'haps ye have me for another. The only man that showed up in the past year was a small, mousey fellow, and he had a girly voice to match."

Sherburn took the bait. He drew himself up. "That *was* me," he replied.

One of the men behind him cleared his throat, another one started to laugh but was silenced by a quick elbow to his side. Sherburn realized his blunder, and his demeanor changed. The deputy squared his shoulders and tried to regain the edge. The wounded man's voice was rising and escalating at a faster clip. Suddenly, he was interrupted.

"Do we have a problem here?" The voice, a deep baritone, would have been pleasant if not delivered in such a menacing fashion. "I don't like disagreements," Benjamin Whiting said. "I've heard about the insolence that the governor's deputies have encountered with settlers livin' deep in the woods. There was one in particular who gave Mr. Sherburn more trouble than most. Would ye know of this man?" His eyes bore into Ebenezer's. As the county's sheriff, he had experienced many confrontations but always maintained the advantage.

Ebenezer realized he was now dealing with the notorious Sheriff Whiting; Whiting had a reputation of abusing his authority to intimidate good, honest people. It was evident he was going to ensure that Ebenezer acknowledged his official capacity.

Without waiting for a response, Whiting unceremoniously pushed Sherburn aside harder than he expected. Sherburn gave a small hop to steady himself; otherwise, he might have ended up on the icy ground. Ebenezer didn't pay him any mind. He was nose to nose with a force of nature.

"*Sheriff* Whiting, your servant sir." Whiting's tone did not match his greeting. "If this deputy came to yer place to do our King's work, he surely did so by King George's command!" he growled. Ebenezer saw that Whiting fancied his position as a badge of honor; it fed his self-esteem. The sheriff puffed out his chest like a cock ready for a fight. When he could not frighten with his physicality, which was formidable, he resorted to threats. Being a sheriff provided him the power to sustain those threats.

"What's yer name?" Whiting demanded. Abruptly, a blast of cold air from the west painted his face in red and white patches as if he were undergoing a sudden allergic reaction. He sniffed several times to prevent his nose from dripping. It appeared he was in the throes of a nasty cold.

Reluctantly, Ebenezer provided the information. He still managed to meet Whiting's glare despite the venom issuing from the sheriff's eyes. Mudgett became aware of the three other men assembling near Whiting, their arms crossed in defiance. It was as though a human wall had started to come between Ebenezer and all reason.

"Well, E-be-*ne*-zer *Mud*-gett," Whiting repeated as if the name were a language foreign to his ears. "I think ye'd better give Mr. Sherburn an apology for yer *contrary* behavior. Ye see, speakin' ill to a governor's deputy is like speakin' ill to the King himself. In England, the prisons are full of people with such ef-*fron*-t'ry." Plumes of mist emanated from his mouth as he spoke, and he finished by wiping his nose with the back of his gloved hand.

"This is far from England and her prisons. We are not bound by the same laws here." Ebenezer's fists clenched at his sides. He tried to match his tone with Whiting's. His typically stolid voice betrayed a slight quiver. A slight smile twitched the corners of the sheriff's lips.

"We *are* bound by such royal laws as . . . the *Pine Tree Law*," he emphasized. "I sure hope yer abidin' *that* one, Mr. Mudgett. I would hate to see Mr. Sherburn here needin' to report ye. The fine and possible imprisonment would be tough for a merchant *or* . . . a *family* man. Ye do have a family, I expect?" He paused and then added slowly, "They would be quite alone fer a bit . . . And who knows *what* could happen to 'em."

The implication was like a fireball landing in the pit of Ebenezer's belly. How dare this man suggest such a thing! Suddenly, his mind was awash in emotions: hatred for the King, indignation for the confounded tree law, concern for Miriam and his children, but most of all at this moment, he despised the intimidating man before him and the threat he enjoyed delivering.

"A man yer age must surely have a houseful of children," he sniffed.

The fireball rose to his chest, and as sweat popped out on his temples, he bellowed, "You'll be leavin' them out of this!" In a flash, he stretched his arms out toward Whiting's shoulders and was about to give the man a hearty push, but someone grabbed him around the waist. The ensuing altercation outside had caught the ears of the Goat's Head tavern-keeper, Daniel. Fortunately, he emerged in the nick of time to prevent Mudgett from laying his hands on Whiting. Ebenezer was pulled back and twisted rapidly to one side. His hat flew off and landed at Whiting's feet. The swift movement and simultaneous jerk not only startled Ebenezer but pushed the air right out of his lungs. The beefy owner of the tavern hung onto Ebenezer as if waiting to see what Whiting's next move would be.

Ebenezer's companions filed out of the tavern to see what was happening. Samuel started to propel himself forward. Caleb stepped in front of him, put his hands out, and shook his head, "Wait!" he warned.

"Yer behavior is indeed very boorish, Mr. Mudgett," the sheriff said too calmly and stooped to pick up Ebenezer's hat. He slapped it against his thigh, ridding it of the snow, and walked over to where Daniel had deposited Ebenezer on the ground, still gasping for air. Whiting put his hand out as a gesture to help him stand up. Cautiously, Ebenezer stretched his hand up to accept it. As soon as he was upright, Whiting whipped the hat across Ebenezer's face. The effort twisted Whiting's body and made him wheeze. The force knocked Ebenezer to the side; Daniel caught him from falling over. Eb crooked his arm up to his face, the back of his hand gingerly touching his cheek; it felt hot and prickly. He squinted his eyes in anger and started to wiggle out of Daniel's grasp. Daniel held him tighter.

"Enough! I'll not have blood spilled and givin' my tavern a bad name! Get on wi' ye and leave each of ye be!" Daniel diffused the conflict with a surprisingly authoritative voice. Even Whiting paid him heed.

He let go of the hold he had on Ebenezer, hoping that the situation had been diffused but afraid to turn his back on Whiting. "Eb, come on in. I'll git ye some flip. The loggerhead has heated a fresh batch—it's all ready fer ye."

Ebenezer sensed that Whiting would not forget this confrontation. His ill-tempered reputation was known throughout the county. Many doubted he performed his duties for the love of law but rather for the enjoyment he reaped from administering the punishment. To Ebenezer, Whiting was just another reason to disparage the Crown. Anyone with authority in England's territory was just the long arm of the King.

Another nagging feeling was wrapping itself tightly around his mind and creating a rhythmic throbbing in his temples, *Sherburn* . . ., that perfidious bastard! It was simply a matter of time before he presented himself at the sawmill. With a sinking feeling, he gulped the flip, burning his tongue. He didn't care. He was too focused on damning the King and his blasted underlings, Sherburn and now Whiting and Quigley!

The Goat's Head Tavern to the Merrimack River

Like Quimby's, the Goat's Head had been in operation long enough to earn a reputation for its comfort and congeniality and was the unofficial gathering place to receive news, gossip, and information. Two long tables comprised of five pine boards, each six inches in width, and equally long pine benches accommodated the weary travelers and thirsty residents of the area who relished swapping stories and conversing. The four round tables seated those who enjoyed playing dominoes or cards while they drank. Unlike the newer taverns that sprang up, Daniel's had a good supply of pewter mugs that hung along the top of the walls. Glass bottles perched on shelves reflected the light of the flickering flames. Wooden pegs under the shelves held the patrons' blue frocks and animal-hide coats. It wasn't uncommon to see a dog curled up near the fire, impervious to the commotion around him.

The men remaining inside the tavern had been bunched up at the window, entertained by the spectacle. As soon as Daniel, Ebenezer, and the other Weare men began to walk toward the door, they scrambled to their original seats. In their rush, the spindle chair legs scraped across the wooden floor. They pretended to be engaged in conversation or resumed their games of dominoes and cards. Ebenezer scanned the room and nodded sheepishly to those facing him. In spite of the inflammation on half of his face, the fire in the hearth drew his attention. He had removed his mittens a half hour ago to throw hay to the oxen, and now he could hardly move his fingers. The fire was a magnet, its warmth drawing him closer. One man twisted in his chair to face him and tried to offer some encouragement.

"Don' ye worry 'bout that Whitin', he comes 'cross as an angry dog, but he's really . . ."

"A man-eating bear!" another interrupted. Soon they all chimed in with their gossip.

"Yeah, even his deputy, that Quigley, is 'fraid o' the beast. When Whiting was yellin' at him, he was shakin' faster 'n a dog after a swim in the Piscataquog!"

Not to be outdone by colorful descriptions, another man added, "He got his orders and flew outta here like a sinner chased by the devil."

"What a clot-head. He expected us to move outta his way. Us with four loaded pungs and teams with nowhere else ta go." Samuel shook his head at the memory.

"Well, Whitin' put the fear o the Lord inta him. He let it be known that Quigley had let 'im down. Ye couldn't help but eavesdrop with his big ole voice bellowin' when he found Quigley in here. Quigley was supposed ta deliver a summons or sumthin and instead the man was here drinkin' and braggin' 'bout this 'n that with no care in the world."

"Ayup, and when the sheriff saw Quigley, he nearly exploded he was so mad."

They all relished telling their stories about John Quigley and fractious Benjamin Whiting, but if their intent was to ease Ebenezer's state of mind, they were not succeeding. He thought that even if many of the accounts were exaggerated, it was evident by his recent experience that much of it was true. The burning sensation on his face where Whiting had slapped him was a not-so-gentle reminder. He was concerned; he could not forget the obvious threat that Whiting made against his family. Whether Ben Whiting meant it or not, Eb knew that he would have to make this journey as quickly as possible so he could return home to Miriam and the children.

The Weare men eyed Ebenezer askance and were of the same mind: It would be prudent to change the subject. Caleb interpreted William's quick lift of his chin as a signal for him to tell one of his stories.

"I met two settlers in a tavern that were havin' an argument over which could bear malice longer, man or woman," Caleb began with a twinkle in his eye. "*Women, of course,* said the one. *Why so?* asked t'other.

Well, he replied, *I had a scuffle with a girl once, and she remembered me for it nine months after!"*

Daniel's wife was standing in the tavern cage, a closet-size enclosure where they stored the spirits. It had a door on the side and a window in front with wooden slats that flipped up and was secured on the ceiling. She leaned on the pine slab at the base of the window and said, while wiping her hands with a rag, "I heard told of a man lookin' just like you, sir, ridin' along near here. He came upon a young woman carryin' a pig in her arms. Hearin' it scream he addressed her thus: *Why my dear, your young child cries amazingly.* The young woman turned around and looked him in the face and said with a smile on her countenance, *I know it, sir. He always does when he sees his daddy!"*

Amid the laughter, Ebenezer and his friends gave Caleb light-hearted claps on his back, and he bowed in subservience to the clever woman. Daniel was used to his wife standing up for womankind. Ebenezer realized over time that Daniel's customers often baited their friends so they could get a dose of her medicine. It was all part of the atmosphere at the Goat's Head.

Ebenezer's posture relaxed. He sank into the nearest chair with his bare feet resting on the fireplace's threshold. The others filled in the empty spaces around the long table in the center of the floor. He concentrated on taking small sips of the steaming flip. The fire popped and wheezed. He closed his eyes and took a long whiff to smell the apples and bran as if the concoction were a mood-enhancing elixir. Jotham had positioned his pot of beans on some coals off to the side, and soon they were filling their bellies, their comfort complete.

After a few uneventful days of travel, they reached the Merrimack River's crossing point, roughly the halfway point to Salem. William Read operated the first ferry in the area, and his headquarters was on the east side of the river, in Litchfield. His least favorite customers in the winter were those with sleds and oxen. It was true the oxen were calmer than horses, but in the winter, if he didn't have help, he had to shovel snow on the gangplank to maneuver a sled onto the flat-bottomed scow. He did not relish doing any more work than necessary; the ferriage alone was taxing on his shoulders. He would have been jealous had he known about the cable pulley system used by an ingenious ferryman in Connecticut. Instead, he was destined to pole the scow from the east to the west and back again, countless times a day, more in the warmer months. After twenty-five years he had provided well for his six children but paid the price in aching shoulders.

The river was broad and deep enough to require the travelers to cross by ferry, but fortunately not so wide that they risked suffering the hazards endured by other colonial-ferry travelers. The waves that splashed up the sides of the scow were never big enough to threaten their safety. On occasion, they might have to wait for strong winds to subside. The river was fast-moving, but still ice build-up this time of the year could delay the operation for days at a time. Read's biggest concern when the ice started to break up was moving the ice floes out of the way. He had found it necessary to hire a boy to help with the pushing. The cheap help never lasted long. Nathaniel, his latest employee, was not always dependable, and Read frequently had to enlist the help of his passengers when he did not show up. This meant having to reduce the fare, which he was very reluctant to do, and only did so when the voyagers complained.

"The blasted redcoats will be here sniffin' around," Jotham explained to Samuel. "The closer to Boston, the more we'll see. On the way back, they'll want to examine our wares, lookin' fer merchandise that disappeared from the docks."

The British redcoats were the visual reminder that the Mother Country had her grip on the colonies. "Well, I fer one am damn glad we don't have ta house any of 'em up where we live. The people 'round here are obliged to take 'em in and feed 'em under the Quartering Act. It's bad enough they interrogate us. I would be outraged havin' one under my roof and eatin' my food!" William said spitting in the snow.

William Read had just transported a minister and his wife with several heavy, loaded crates destined for their new church. He was waiting on the west side landing before heading back, hoping to rest his weary body and to wait for potential eastbound passengers. He massaged his right shoulder and moved it in circles to loosen the joint. Through squinted eyes, he saw several teams of oxen heading in his direction. He craned his neck to count the teams and cursed out loud.

"Four trips back-to-back. I'll be back directly," Read said over his shoulder to Nathaniel and started to jog to McGaw's Tavern where a hot drink could fortify him. On the way, he smirked and said out loud, "Those men won't be goin' anywhere. They'll stay put 'til I return."

Nathaniel waited for his employer to disappear, shrugged, and wandered off.

By the time Read returned, the men were jumping in place and clapping their frozen hands. He greeted them brusquely with a wave of his arm and looked around for Nathaniel. "That puddin'-headed fellow!" he said under his breath and grabbed the shovel off the scow. "He doesn't know how to do a full day's work without whinin' or skippin' out on me!" He leaned on the shovel and barked to the men, "Ten shillings fer the trip per team, man, and sled, paid before the trip begins."

The men nodded; it wasn't their first time crossing with William Read. Ebenezer frowned when the man acted as if he had never seen them before. His intuitive nature sensed that Read was not only mad at his young helper but annoyed with them for some reason. He watched as Read balanced the shovel against his leg and rubbed his shoulder. Without saying a word, he took the shovel from the ferryman's hands and started heaving the snow onto the apron of the scow.

And so the long process began, loading one team at a time, crossing the river, and returning for the next one. Each man stood ready with the pole to push away any ice floes that threatened to interfere with the crossing. Jotham and his team were the last to cross. He spread a new layer of snow on the apron, more to disguise the gangplank that would intimidate his young oxen, than to help the pung slide. He returned to one side of the team and commanded, "Move on!" The team responded by snorting and sending small plumes of mist into the air while attempting to back up. Jotham snapped the goad on both the rumps and repeated the command. No advancement.

All the others were watching on the opposite landing. They had already endured the two redcoats' interrogation about their cargo and suspicious circling of their pungs by rolling their eyes behind the soldiers' backs, grunting, and exchanging looks of disgust. Jotham was left alone to entice the beasts to move onto the scow's apron. Even with the goad, the bigger steer pulled his companion to the right to avoid moving forward. Read, mollified by the travelers' help in shoveling the snow for him and shoving the ice chunks away, broke his long-held rule to refrain from aiding to load animals. He picked up the shovel and stood next to the stronger ox's head, miming to the beast he was ready to administer a whack if he dared to turn toward him. Jotham held the pole in his left hand by the other ox's head and snapped the goad in the other hand. Both men yelled, "Move on!" Read gave his ox a quick wallop on the rump and the beasts moved forward. Finally, after getting positioned on the scow, the team expressed their displeasure with several bellows. When the scow started to float, they stomped in place with every bump and dip.

A Seed is Planted

A few days later they arrived at Richard Derby's wharf under an unusually warm, late-January sun. The pungent smells wafted and tangled in the air like invisible strands of a woman's hair blown about in a high wind. The steaming horse and oxen manure entwined with the smell of salty sea air and, even in the winter, the smell of fish seemed to emanate from the damp wood. Screeching seagulls perched on rooftops or circled overhead. Their piercing screams reminded Ebenezer of the wounded animals he hunted in the woods. The cries of agony were indistinguishable from the cries of these hungry birds warning their feathered friends not to venture too close to their prospective food sources. Those familiar with the gulls knew to conceal food in their hands, or a tasty morsel could be skillfully plucked from fingers in seconds.

The cold winter months were not as frenetic on the wharf as the warmer ones, but plenty of activity abounded. No less than twenty structures lined the busy wharf, the longest in Salem. At the beginning of the pier was the stately red-brick Custom House, at the end was the Derby Wharf Lighthouse. The structures in between were a combination of shacks and three-story warehouses. Vessels purged load after load of materials and goods brought from distant ports. Horses and oxen, a few bystanders, sailors, merchants, and dockhands moved in all different directions. In spite of the winter season, vessels had continued to arrive, reaching their destination later than predicted due to harsh ocean storms or, simply, navigational error.

Most notable was the sight of several red uniforms visible at both ends of the wharf. For the past four years, the British soldiers patrolling the wharf had used Writs of Assistance to crack down on smuggling. The written command gave the soldiers legal authority to search for contraband any time or place and to use any manner of search. While some soldiers were engaged in performing the inspections of the merchandise coming and going, others collected taxes. Children who had escaped the clutches of their parents delighted in throwing jeers and insults in the soldiers' direction until the nervous mothers hushed the youngsters and whisked them away.

Ebenezer's friends dispersed to other parts of the wharf to do their bartering. He maneuvered his oxen directly to the Derby Distillery where he was anxious to receive compensation for his wares, get the rum and supplies, and embark on his return home. He was pleased with the thirty-gallon barrels he had fashioned;

they were much easier to handle and transport than the hefty 110-gallon hogsheads commonly used in the West Indies.

Ebenezer's mind drifted to past events. He could not stop dwelling on the encounter with Whiting. The cheerful sun's rays did nothing to dispel the onerous, sour mood he couldn't shake. Even his good fortune to have acquired more rum this trip in exchange for his bartered goods had little effect.

The people who inhabited the community of the North Shore were somewhat oblivious to the Pine Tree Law. Little did they know, or seem to care, how it was obstructing the progress and hampering the peace of their northern neighbors' existence in the wilderness. They had different bones of contention with the Mother Country.

The Boston Massacre had occurred two years prior. British soldiers killed five Patriots in retaliation for the stones and snowballs they threw at them. Six British soldiers had been acquitted and two more given reduced sentences, exacerbating the colonists' sensitivity to the royal presence. Additionally, they were still harboring ill will concerning the Townshend Acts, recently repealed by Parliament. The Townshend Acts had forced the colonists to pay tariffs on items from Britain that had been manufactured using the colonists' own natural resources. In spite of the repeal, Britain was not going to keep its greedy fingers out of their business. As a result, colonial assemblies were bubbling to the surface all over the North Shore. The assemblies were elected by the people and served as advocates for their interests before royal authorities. The Massachusetts House of Representatives reached out to the assemblies to join the resistance and boycott the merchants importing the British goods.

Charles, an obsequious free black man, hired by the distillery, helped Ebenezer load his pung with the precious barrels of rum. Ebenezer and Charles had established a friendship of sorts by means of a common dislike for the redcoats. On a previous trip, Ebenezer had rescued Charles from the receiving end of their insults and rough treatment. Ever since that day, Charles was the dockworker who always rushed to help Ebenezer when he and his team showed up on the wharf. In all the time Ebenezer had known him, he might have heard a total of a dozen words from the white-haired man. The majority were "Yessir."

Suddenly chaos erupted all around them on the busy wharf. Nearby, there was a fight underway in front of the Customs House. Charles seemed impervious to the verbal venom spilling out into the air and continued hoisting the barrels as if the conflict were a daily occurrence. Ebenezer, momentarily freed from the haunting of recent events, stopped and tried to hear the nature of the fuss. Then an angry shout from the opposite direction from the Custom House diverted his attention. One of the dockhands, pushing a cart precariously stacked with barrels of molasses, had cried out. A rider had been unable to control his agitated horse, and the nervous animal had backed into the dockhand's wheelbarrow. The weight of the barrels shifted to one side as he attempted to avoid the frightened horse. He was unable to stabilize the heavy barrels. The handles twisted from his grasp. The wayward barrels proceeded to roll in all different directions.

Havoc and confusion reigned on the wharf. Several people either attempted to dodge the runaway cargo or tried to stop the barrels before they injured someone. The casks knocked people into each other, creating a domino effect on the congested wharf. One of the barrels, bleeding its thick, sticky ooze of molasses, hit a post and was thrust sideways. It caught a British soldier off guard. It scaled up his body to his knees and rolled back down again, but not before it left him cursing on the ground with a trail of brown sludge on his uniform. The people affected by the runaway barrels yelled and cursed. Those out of harm's way laughed and pointed. A large, rough-looking man emerged from the distillery's warehouse and began admonishing the dockhand who had lost control of his cart. The dockhand pleaded his innocence and subsequently reeled around to swear at the horse's rider. Soon the turmoil was confined to just the two of them.

When the tide of pandemonium started to ease, Ebenezer, safe from any danger, turned back to his pung in time to catch a glimpse of Charles biting his bottom lip. The liquor merchant sensed Charles was struggling to conceal the growing smile on his dark face. Previous experience had apparently taught the black man to contain his emotions. Charles bowed his head, shook it several times, and got back to business.

Ebenezer's thoughts returned to his own affairs. He looked around to be sure there were no soldiers or possible Loyalists within earshot and grumbled under his breath again about the King and the horrid tree law. Even though he did not expect Charles to respond, he considered him a safe sounding board. He described the invasion of his land, Sherburn, and Whiting's threat, omitting the detail about hacking out the King's Broad Arrow from his trees. After describing Quigley's insolence on the trail, Mudgett stopped short. He sensed someone standing nearby. He looked up. A nicely dressed gentleman leaning on his cane was listening intently to the one-sided conversation.

The elderly gentleman quickly scanned Mudgett from head to toe. He then glanced at the team and the pung in the process of being stacked high with barrels and other goods.

"I suspect you have arrived from a long distance. Am I correct in assuming you are from the wilds of New Hampshire, sir?"

"You assume correctly, sir." Ebenezer did not stop working. "And I assume you are not." His tone reflected the irritation he felt for the surveillance.

The man smiled and ignored Ebenezer's curt reply. "I feel you have reason to harbor ill will, friend. Those such as I may not share your rancor for the same reason but share an equal distaste for England for imposing similar restrictions on our livelihood," he said quietly. Ebenezer narrowed his eyes. The stranger peered over his spectacles as if looking for validation of their commonality.

The well-dressed man scrutinized both directions of the wharf. When he concluded it was safe, he stepped closer. He lowered his voice to alert Ebenezer to the importance of the message he was about to deliver. He stated cryptically, "If some of the pups refuse to suckle, the bitch may suffer."

Ebenezer wondered if he had heard correctly, then, grasping the analogy, responded in a firm voice, "But... She might bite her pups in return, or worse... Devour 'em." He continued to hoist the barrels with Charles.

The gentleman, undeterred by Ebenezer's apparent dismissal, smiled again and raised his hirsute eyebrows to emphasize his words, "Perhaps, but if *all* the pups refuse to suckle, she undoubtedly *will* suffer. It is important for *all* pups to engage in making the message stronger."

Ebenezer paused. He put the barrel down with a thud. With his hands on his hips, he turned to face the gentleman. "Are you suggesting... *resistance*, sir?" Ebenezer's voice remained low but firm. He hid his shock at the reference to... *resistance*.

"I am only pointing out that action has already taken place with beneficial results. Although we have experienced some success, the *mother* is still applying force. There are many litters anxious to take action, but we need them *all* to engage for the benefit of *all*. The mother will feel the pressure."

He moved even nearer and bent his head next to Mudgett's ear and whispered, "In Boston . . . I heard someone quoting Benjamin Franklin: *The first responsibility of every citizen is to question authority*; we have done that and have witnessed results. You must know that the Townshend Duties were repealed, thanks to our efforts. Indeed, why was it equitable for us to pay taxes on products that were made with *our* natural resources that we sent to England? It was not, sir. We should be our own nation, governed by our own, not by some removed sovereign who taxes us for the benefit of the land where *he* resides and gives us no representation in return."

Ebenezer noted that the impassioned man's voice was rising steadily. He was relieved to see the man taking a step backward. The gentleman lowered his chin into the clean white stock, took a deep breath, and once again peered over his spectacles to silently assess Ebenezer's reaction.

"I will take what ye have said under advisement, sir. I appreciate yer candor," Ebenezer stated decisively, expecting to put an end to the conversation. The man's sanguine disclosures were making him uneasy—a British soldier could appear at any minute.

"Here in Massachusetts," the man continued, "we have prepared a statement of colonists' rights as men,

Christians, and subjects. We call it the Boston Pamphlet, and it outlines the violations of recent British policies. We have been doing more than question, sir. Patrick Henry is leading the Sons of Liberty, a secret organization of stouthearted men committed to rousing the sensibilities of our *mother*," he emphasized. "Resistance through agitation has brought results. It appears to me that you and, may I surmise, others like yourself may be following Franklin's advice. Perhaps now it is time for action, *hmmm*?" He moved his cane out, creating a three-point triangle with his polished boots, and leaned on it with both hands.

Ebenezer frowned. The man pushed himself upright as though possessed by a sudden idea. He unbuttoned his frock and fished around inside. He glanced up and down the wharf before pulling out a folded paper. He smiled, "Here, ye can see what I mean by this." He low-handed it to Mudgett.

"*The Massachusetts Spy*?" Eb whispered and frowned above the pamphlet at the gentleman. He started to scan the document while the man explained.

"Isaiah Thomas is an intrepid young printer who has been using his newspaper to rally support for the cause of *independence*." At the mention of independence, Eb looked up. For the last several years, each time the liquor merchant had made his journey for supplies, he had heard grumblings against the Crown. This was the first time he had been approached to take action, and it was the first time he had heard anything about separation from British rule.

"Isaiah also publishes handbills for the Sons of Liberty. He has arranged for special post riders to exchange news and papers with like-minded citizens of other colonies. The stories of British abuses have stirred up anger in a good many colonies. Perhaps ye shall have something for him to add in his next publication, hmm? He has a considerable circulation." He paused for effect. "Isaiah has put his personal liberty at stake but has exposed the abuses nevertheless. It is through such boldness that we are making progress."

Charles heaved the last barrel onto the pung, the oxen shifted in place, and Ebenezer's attention turned toward the black man. He nodded to acknowledge Charles's wordless farewell and watched him disappear into the warehouse. He wondered if the recent conversation had had any effect on the impassive ex-slave. He turned back to address the stranger once more. He had disappeared as well. Eb noticed a British soldier heading down the wharf in his direction. He quickly stuffed the paper between two casks. He was left alone for a few more moments to contemplate the nature of the recent discourse.

Ebenezer was standing with his head down, staring at the wooden wharf boards and frowning when William approached him.

"Ye feelin' right, Eb? Ye look a bit lost."

"I've got a lot ta think about, William. Maybe it's time we do something." William simply stared back with a quizzical look.

"We'll get ourselves to the Daniels House," Mudgett continued, "where we can talk. I can't say much now, and I want to wait for the others."

A Conversation Begins

The Daniels House was built in 1667 and continued to be operated by a Daniels descendant, as it would be for another two centuries. It was everyone's favorite destination in Salem before heading back home. The men would have the only prepared suppers on the journey and would spend one or two nights there. They treated it as a kind of celebration. Mrs. Daniels's reputation as an excellent cook was well-known. Of course, she had the advantage of being a short walk from the Derby Wharf, where her housemaid had the opportunity to buy the freshest fish and the most exotic spices.

Ebenezer knew that a British soldier quartered here could appear at any moment. To avoid anyone from overhearing the discussion he planned to have with his friends, he had convinced Mistress Daniels to allow them to use the private dining room away from the barroom. It was closed off in the colder months, being a distance from a heat source and on the northern side of the house that bore the brunt of the winter winds. What it lacked in warmth would be made up in privacy. During the warmer months, Mrs. Daniels fed many Patriots holding their clandestine meetings in this room to debate their ideas against the government.

There was always enough food to feed twice as many of them. Servant girls distributed steaming plates of boiled potatoes loaded with butter, platters of roast beef and veal with gravy, several loaves of bread, salted fish in cream sauce, hasty pudding and milk, and lastly, sweet cake and some pies. The men leaned forward in their straight-back chairs and inhaled the aroma of each platter as the girls slid them on the table; then they dug in as if they hadn't eaten in days.

"I don't know if Caleb's cheeks are gettin' redder from eyein' the food or the ones bringin' it!" laughed William.

"Well, William, I hope you're eyein' the food. Ye've got a long way to go to put meat on yer bones. I think yer wife would curse ye if t'were the women that made ye hungry!" Jotham poked William in the ribs. He was one of the few who could tease William about his wife's reputation as a witch.

The men's spirits were always high when they broke bread here, and except for Ebenezer, they were all laughing and sharing their stories of the day. Ebenezer fidgeted with his stock. He started to pace the pumpkin-pine floor, its warm orange color produced from a century of foot traffic entering and departing the room. He knew anything serious would not be popular, but he wanted to discuss the mysterious Salem man while it was still fresh in his mind. He cleared his throat. His friends were too absorbed in conversation and helping themselves to the feast to notice. He picked up his pewter plate and smacked it down on the table. Then Ebenezer nodded toward the door and eyed William, who reluctantly rose to close it. He had their attention.

Eb ran his fingers through his hair like a comb and then moved his index finger back and forth across the stubble on his chin. He chose his words carefully. "We have been pushed around too long. Ye know what happened at the Goat's Head and before that on the road with Quigley. This happens all the time now. We are being subjected to the King's administrators' insults and abuses. Because of the King, we are slowly losin' what we have worked so hard to build. Our families are going to suffer for it."

"What do you think we can do, Eb? We're just a bunch of woodsmen, settlers. Ye want us ta shoot 'em?" Jotham laughed. The brisk weather had deepened his ruddy complexion and accentuated his blue eyes.

Ebenezer spoke in a measured tone, "I'm not saying anything about *shooting*. I'm saying *resistance*. I'm saying we aren't alone in this. The other colonies have been *organizing*, and in our neck of the woods, we should also." He continued in a faster clip, "Everybody in the town here, and even our Portsmouth, was up in arms about the Stamp Act. Well, we didn't waste a lot of gripin' time on that, but they did, and it got repealed by colonies bandin' together. We despise the Pine Tree Law. It may mean few beans to them here, but we need to let them know how it is affectin' us. Don't ye see? All taxes and laws without any representation are unjust. More will be comin' from across the ocean to replace the ones that just got repealed. We don't get any say in this. We pay, and England gives us *nothing*—they just take from us." He paused. "Resistance with agitation works."

"Ebenezer, we have known about this fer a long time. Why are ye hot under the collar now?" Jotham asked. He was soon rewarded with the details of the well-dressed man's words and the hope they implied.

"He told me of the assemblies that have met, the articles that have been written. He said that people have been organizin' for a while now." He lowered his voice and added, "The Sons of Liberty is a secret organization that has made the Crown listen." He pulled Isaiah Thomas's *Massachusetts Spy* out from under his coat and waved it in the air. "This is unitin' the people in their shared concerns!" He passed it around the table.

William was fussing with the bones in his fish when he said, "There are a lot more people here in Massachusetts to *organize*. We are scattered all over the woods. How do you expect us to *organize*?"

"We should be meetin' on a regular schedule. I will have to ask more questions, get more answers, let others know we are startin' to question authority as

Benjamin Franklin wants us to do. We . . ."

"Benjamin Franklin!!" Caleb interrupted. "Well now, are ye havin' tea with ole Ben and helpin' him write his *Poor Richard's Almanac?*" Caleb laughed. Samuel started to ask who Poor Richard was but decided to save it for later.

Ebenezer was determined to keep them focused on the seriousness of his report. He glared at Caleb and continued, "If we continue to meet, share our concerns, and reach out to others, we will get stronger, we will grow. I'm sayin' we have to be open to resist. Otherwise, families won't be able to survive as the King puts more restrictions on us." He looked over at Samuel who was deep in thought. The poor fellow was going to have a hard time even starting a family without the means to pay for the license on his trees, and then not be able to cut down the most useful ones to build his cabin. The mention of family also reminded Eb that he couldn't afford to remain in Salem a day longer.

"I've got ta leave early and get back to the sawmill." Eb cleared his throat and admitted after a cautious pause, "I hacked out the royal mark on some trees I felled. I know it was foolish. It won't protect me and could grant me a bigger fine. I could even go to prison. After I get them sawed, I'll need ta hide them or else they'll confiscate 'em and make me pay." Then attempting to brush over his revelation, he continued. "But then I want ta speak with Abraham and the Worthley brothers and some others about this." He pointed with his knife to the *Massachusetts Spy*, currently in front of Jotham.

The sound of cutlery striking the pewter plates ceased. Samuel lifted his head and stared wide-eyed and open-mouthed at Ebenezer. The partly chewed veal almost slipped out. "Ye are the one that warned me not to cut my pines! And ye destroyed the King's Broad Arrow on them?"

With heads still bent over their plates, the others were just pushing their food around and looking much like chastised little boys. Samuel looked at each man. Not one returned Samuel's glance nor seemed shocked at Mudgett's declaration.

After a brief silence, Samuel blurted out, "Ye *all*, ye *all* are guilty!"

William was the first to speak up, "Well, I'm not goin' to let it interfere with my fun here. I'm stayin' tomorrow, at least, and then will head back. Sherburn has a lot of towns to cover and the chance he'll make it back to Weare in the next two weeks is slight. What about you fellas?"

Caleb didn't hesitate to agree with William. Ebenezer was not surprised when Caleb raised his tankard up and toward William as if he were giving him a toast. "I see no hurry. I'm not sayin' we don't have ta be careful about our logs, but I'm not rushin' back while I still have business here. I'm still workin' on a good trade fer Worthley's hides. As far as resistance goes, Eb, I'm not sure what ye mean by it, or what we could do."

"Me neither," Jotham said. "We can't take on the British soldiers. Even if we picked off a few, more would be comin' 'cross the water. The loyalty to the Crown runs deep, and I don't want to run up against that Tory . . . *Whiting*."

"Yes, there exists loyalty to the King, Jotham, but only for those who benefit from it. Ye can see by the paper in front of ye that there are more who, like us, are not happy with few rights to our own property. I'm just sayin' we keep ourselves ready if a situation presents itself. Keep yer ears open and don't be afraid to show support if it is needed." He remembered the bravado they showed at Quimby's Inn, albeit under the influence of several mugs of Aaron's flip, and wished they were showing a modicum of it now.

Samuel's head was turning left and right to follow the conversation. He looked confused and concerned about what he was learning.

"What about my land? Am I the fool fer wantin' to homestead in the northeast? Should I follow yer advice that ye didn't even take yerselves? How can I build the kind of cabin I want without trees of decent size? What do you mean about *resisting*?" All the men ignored his questions; no one knew how to answer them.

"What do ye mean, 'if a situation presents itself?'" William was getting agitated.

"I don't know, William!" Ebenezer raised his voice and then lowered it. "I just know that it's been happenin' here. Like the man told me, secret committees have been formed, more groups are startin' to protest, letters are being written. The Crown is beginnin' to pay attention or the Stamp and Townshend Acts wouldn't have been repealed."

"I still don't know what we can do," Caleb said.

"Wait!" Ebenezer met the eyes of each man and hissed, "Just wait and stay ready!"

The awkward silence that followed gave way to the sounds of meat ripped off knives and chewed, but less voraciously than when they started. Ebenezer was hoping he had convinced them, but at the very least, he had given them something to think about. *Perhaps that is all I can hope for now*, he thought.

The discourse had put a damper on the evening; the men seemed to resent Ebenezer for it, and he resented their meek reactions. William had changed the subject, but the damage to the earlier lighthearted atmosphere was done. After eating in silence, Ebenezer retired early with the excuse of having to leave before dawn. He wanted to get a good start on the journey back. He would be making the return trip alone.

An Unwelcome Visitor

"Ma-MA!"

Miriam knew Sarah was about to complain bitterly about some horrible, terrible act a younger sibling was inflicting upon her. According to Sarah, Jesse, William, or young Miriam were always targeting her and her alone. *I don't know why I should be surprised*, Miriam thought, *my daughter has a way of inviting others to torment her.* Miriam gave an exasperated shake of her head to Claire, who was seated at the kitchen table near the fire cutting up potatoes. With Ebenezer gone, the door to his office at the end of the kitchen had been shut to keep more warmth from the big fireplace from escaping. It would have been enjoyable without the hollering coming from one of the front rooms.

"MAMA!" Sarah screamed again. "Tell Jesse to stop pullin' on my thread!"

"Daughter, can ye not tell him that yerself?" she tried to speak in a measured tone, knowing that raising her voice would only precipitate more severe whining. She could not tolerate whining. This was a rare moment when she was glad her husband was not there to offer some misplaced solace to placate Sarah. She felt that only encouraged the children to bring their minor differences to their parents' attention, rather than solving situations on their own.

"He's still pullin', Mama. Help! Jesse, leave me BE!! Let go! MAMA!" The rambunctious three-year-old was laughing and squealing with delight. One end of the brown thread was gripped securely in his little hands. The opposite end was embedded in a sampler that Sarah was clutching to her chest.

"I don't see that ye are tryin' too hard to stop his antics, Daughter. Are ye sure ye aren't pleased to be usin' yer little brother as an excuse for less than satisfactory handiwork?"

Miriam stood in the doorway of the large room. Ever since it held the first town assembly in Weare, they had called it the meeting room. She watched the tussle with amusement. She had quickly deduced that her lovely brown-headed daughter could easily have loosened the thread from her much younger brother's grip. Sarah had made it known to anyone within earshot that she despised doing the cross-stitch, and her work showed it. Miriam thought she would have a relatively decent excuse for this afternoon's slipshod work.

"Mother, stop laughing," she pleaded. "Jesse is impossible!"

Encouraged by his mother's enjoyment, Jesse's giggles increased. He began to hop and jump as he pulled on the thread. His sister was not amused and responded by hastily yanking the thread, which then propelled him into her lap, nose meeting nose. Jesse held his breath as if to evaluate her reaction before allowing himself to respond. His bug-eyed expression staring into her eyes was too much for Sarah to resist, and she burst out laughing.

"Ye wee toad, you're not worth a button!" She said, tickling Jesse until he squirmed and writhed off her lap. She followed him to the floor and straddled him, so her long hair fell about his face and into his mouth. "How do you like that, brother?" She laughed. She held his hands down, limiting his resistance to whipping his face left and right. He began to hiccup between the gales of laughter, which made his sister laugh even harder. She would have continued until he whimpered for mercy, but Ezra stormed into the house. As was her custom, Miriam would have complained about him tracking in snow, but his wide-eyed expression likened him to a frightened animal. She waited for him to speak.

"Mother, there's a man outside," Ezra warned. "He was askin' if father was still gone." He left the door open wide enough for Miriam to see a sour-faced man on a handsome black horse facing the house. The wind lifted the horse's forelock out of its eyes, allowing the polished silver on his bridle to gleam in the light. She gathered her shawl, wrapping it tightly around her shoulders, and headed for the door. It wasn't unusual for a stranger to stop and ask for assistance or to try to sell something. Living on the main road lent itself to helping others, and they were always willing to provide whatever help they could. But this stranger knew Ebenezer was away. Ezra put a hand out to warn her, "He isn't very friendly actin'." Miriam glanced at her son and saw the concerned look in his eyes. She looked out the door. She smiled to reassure him. He appeared a man not without means. In spite of his countenance, she felt he offered no threat to their well-being.

"Stay here. I'm sure there's no reason to fuss. Put another log on the fire and ask Claire to mind the little children fer a minute." She suddenly wondered if something might have happened to her husband. The winter trips were a lot easier for him when he was younger.

"Tis a fine afternoon, sir. Are ye in need of some help? She shielded her eyes from the low winter sun as she approached him. Miriam ran her fingers along the horse's strong, muscled neck.

The man peered down at her, put the back of his gloved hand to his mouth, and emitted a long series of coughs. The last hack rendered him gasping for air. When the spasm ceased, Miriam noted the unkind eyes that peeked out from under his woolen cap. He cleared his throat and growled an introduction.

"Benjamin Whiting, Sheriff of the County, your servant, mistress." He paused for effect. "It's a cold day, Mistress Mudgett. I'm in want of a warm drink before I head south." He started coughing again, this time the attack nearly rocked him off the saddle. While he was momentarily distracted, she took the opportunity to evaluate his appearance: fine wool cloak, polished leather boots, leather gloves, well-fed horse. She had no reason to doubt he was who he said he was, but his rough attitude was disquieting. *And how did he know my name?*

"Sir, perhaps ye would be more comfortable across the way to Quimby's Inn. They have a continuous loggerhead warmin' up some flip. We only have some cider," she lied. She barely got her words out when he dismounted with a grunt and started tying his horse to the post.

"Sheriff Whiting, sir. Certainly, the rum at Quimby's would taste better and ease yer coughin'."

He headed to the door as though he were a regular visitor. She had to quicken her step to keep up with him. Miriam gripped her shawl tighter to her chest and ran in front of him before he reached the front stoop. She quickly hopped up so she could look down at him. She mustered all the authority in her voice that was possible, all the while wishing her husband would miraculously appear.

"Please sir, I must insist . . ." he thrust his arm out and shoved her to the side.

He used the same hand to push open the door. It banged against the wall. He strolled dramatically into the room. The thick heels of his boots struck against the wide polished floorboards as though announcing his presence and signaling his authority. He strode past the children on the wool hearth rug and went directly to the roaring fire. Whiting put the toe of one boot onto the hearth and leaned in closer, rubbing his hands together to get the full benefit of the warmth. Young Miriam and Jesse ran to their mother and clutched at her skirts. William hid behind Sarah. Ezra turned toward Miriam to register her reaction. She gave him a quick reassuring smile but walked between Whiting and John, sleeping peacefully in his cradle.

"What is it ye want with us, sir?" she said as she scooped John up and held him close. The baby made a gurgling sound but didn't wake.

Claire, alerted by the unease in her mistress's voice, emerged from the kitchen. She stood in the doorway, the fingers of one hand pinching her bottom lip. Her mistress's tone was frightening her. Achsah peered from behind her.

Miriam caught the lascivious glance the sheriff directed at Sarah. Miriam had seen boys Sarah's age steal fleeting looks her way, but this was different. His eyes were slowly scanning her daughter from top to toe. Sarah turned to her mother with a look of fear. Miriam cleared her throat and repeated the question louder. Again, the man ignored her.

He started to concentrate on the fine details of the Mudgett house. He studied the beautifully hewn mantel, the exquisite workmanship in the posts and beams. The wood used for the walls was chestnut. Miriam knew he was thinking chestnut was hardly the choice for a man of modest means. She watched him survey the silver candlesticks. The furniture was not the crudely fashioned pieces he saw in many settlers' homes. He peered into the dining room next to the meeting room and in front of the kitchen. Most Weare houses didn't have a dining room; people ate in their kitchens if they had one. As he slowly but purposefully took long strides around the rooms, he made sounds as if he were there to evaluate everything inside. With hands on his hips, Whiting hesitated and looked up the stairs that separated the two front rooms. Miriam thought he was about to go up.

"Ye mentioned cider did ye not?" he coughed out.

Ezra, fancying himself the man of the house, with his father gone and Moses out hunting, started to walk toward him but Miriam caught her son's cloak with trembling fingers and pulled him backward. He would undoubtedly have exacerbated the situation.

"Certainly, sir. T'will only take a minute. The cider is hot already." Miriam spread her free arm out to guide her children and gently pressure them toward the kitchen. Claire instinctively took the baby from Miriam. The children stood close to their mother as she started to retrieve the copper pot from the open hearth.

"Mama, does he mean to harm us?" young Miriam whispered. "Why is he here? Does he know Papa?"

"No, dear hearts, he's just sick. He's feelin' poorly and surely he's just tired and cold.

"I should say he's sick," Sarah offered.

"He'll have his cider and be on his way." Her

soothing whispers belied her concern. She was sure he was here for something besides cider.

"I can look for Moses. I know where he's huntin' deer. I'll tell him to bring his gun."

"No, no, Ezra!" she said quickly. "That won't be necessary!" and she smiled at the two youngest ones as though it were a joke. She bunched up her apron to protect her hand. She removed the pot from the swinging crane and poured the steaming cider into the mug. She poured it just half full.

"Ezra, did you finish bringing in the wood?" She tilted her head and used her chin to point outside. He tightened his bottom lip and reluctantly shook his head.

Feigning cheerfulness, she addressed William. "I'll be back directly. Give a twist to the roast; I'll baste it when I return." She hoped to give him and the others a sense of normalcy.

Generally, William would have protested. Miriam knew he disliked twisting the roasted meat almost as much as Sarah disliked doing her cross-stitch. It was a boring job, and William usually was able to bribe Achsah to do it for him. She drew in a deep breath, expecting him to argue. He gave her a look that eased her breathing, and she returned it with a quick, small smile, giving him credit for sensing that this was not the time to protest. He twisted the thick hempen string around several times. He joined his siblings near the doorway to monitor the conversation before he had to twist it again.

The sheriff had found the iron pipe tongs and was

fishing in the coals for one small enough to light his pipe. He ignored Miriam standing near him until he managed to get the pipe lit. The long process forced Miriam to set the mug down on the hearth. She took a few steps back, smoothed down her apron, and shook a wisp of hair from her eyes. The silence engulfed them.

"How do ye know my good husband?" She finally inquired.

"Good? Mistress Mudgett, yer husband threatened my very person," he narrowed his eyes and bore into her surprised ones. "His imprudence toward our King George will not be tolerated."

At the mention of the King, Miriam's head made a small jerk backward as she inhaled a quick breath. She bit her bottom lip, frowned, and waited for an explanation.

"Ye need manners on the road. Yer husband is wantin' in that respect."

"I fear you must be mistaken. My *good* husband is a law abidin' man. He is an admired and respected leader in our town. Many seek his council; he was a constable," she babbled.

He blew on the hot beverage which instigated another coughing fit. In between coughs he took small sips and the coughing finally subsided. Miriam fumbled with her apron, not sure what she should do next. She did not expect what followed.

Whiting took a last sip of the cider and put the mug on the mantel. Then he dumped the burning tobacco from his pipe back into the fireplace and twisted his mouth into a wry smile. He looked at Miriam as his hand touched the corner of his cap then turned and faced the frightened children hovering near the kitchen doorway. The movement caused them to take a synchronized step backward. He touched his hat again but concentrated his gaze on Sarah. She shuffled uncomfortably and wrapped her shawl tighter around her chest. "Good day, children," Whiting sneered.

"Mistress Mudgett, be sure to tell Mr. Mudgett I came to call on ye. Good day," and gave a slight bow that looked more like a mock than courtesy.

His sardonic smile dissipated by the time he reached the door. When he was a safe distance away, the younger children rushed to encircle their perplexed mother. They grabbed at her skirts and peered up at her, waiting for reassurance that everything was all right. Her hands answered by reaching down and hugging two of them closer as she watched the intrusive man slowly mount his black horse.

"Mother, what was that all about? Do you think father is alright?" Achsah asked, peering out the window.

"No need to fret. Father is fine. He would have said otherwise."

Moses entered a few minutes later with his gun in one hand and an empty sack in the other. His eyes darted from person to person as he registered that something was troubling everyone. He joined Achsah at the window and tried to discern the identity of the man leaving their property. "Mother, who was that man?" He said it louder than he intended and woke the baby in Claire's arms. "Did something happen to father?" he asked amid the wailing.

Whiting trotted over to Quimby's Inn. He would drink some warm flip, get a good night's sleep, and then leave for his home right after daybreak. He was smiling like a man that had accomplished his mission.

Homeward Bound

The stranger's words on the wharf swirled around in Ebenezer's mind. The need to clear a few small branches off the trail provided a welcome interlude. As much as the man's implication made him uncomfortable, he could not erase it. He knew the gentleman was right; something had to be done, but he felt the same issues did not confront them. He was fairly certain no one in Massachusetts would head for the northern woods to aid them in support of resistance to the Pine Tree Law. He silently laughed at the thought of the settlers rising up against the organized British power: A couple of pitch forks and axes confronting trained battalions of troops with rifles? Hardly an equal match!

Yet, the nagging thought, *litters* are ready.... What if there really were many impassioned groups willing to act in *all* the colonies? Already an angry mob in Portsmouth had burned the tax collector, George Meserve, in effigy. Ebenezer remembered the banner hanging in the town center, "Liberty, Property, No Stamp." Meserve was made to renounce his commission and to take an oath not to perform his duties; a few months later the Stamp Act was repealed. Last year there was the skirmish in Boston against the British soldiers. He was still uneasy about the confrontations with Sherburn and Whiting; now his mind was occupied by something more dangerous—following the man's suggestion to resist authority. He needed to hurry home and discuss this with his other friends, and Miriam.

He could hear the comforting roar of the Amoskeag Falls on the road to Goffstown, signaling he was but a two-day's journey from home. He missed Miriam and the children more than he ever had on other trips. Abruptly, he was aware that the rumbling was not just the cascading water.

Ahead, coming down the Mast Road, he could discern the first row of the oxen teams straining as they pulled another massive white pine log. Its destiny was to stand erect once more, adorned not with its powerful limbs and greenery, but with the billowing sails of a British naval ship sailing in far-off seas to protect the British Empire. An empire for which Ebenezer felt little connection.

The commands and rough encouragement shouted out by dozens of men amidst the grunting of tens of oxen teams grew louder. Despite the repulsion for what he believed to be thievery on the part of the King, he could not help but feel awestruck every time he witnessed the hauling. Sweat, manure, and the sap bleeding from the tree's amputation aroused his sense of smell; the ground shook under his feet as scores of hooves dug deep in the earth. Row after row of oxen teams passed until Ebenezer saw the great wheels, called the mast wheels. The wheels were nine feet in diameter with six-inch iron tires, a pair in front and back. Each wheel weighed a thousand pounds. In between, stretched the victim.

His admiration for the engineering feat did not linger long. It would delay him a bit. Eb realized today's hauling would carve great ruts into the road, making the execution around the furrows challenging. He had no other choice but to wait for the procession to pass, and then he could be on his way.

When he was able to continue, he noticed the wind had picked up on the trail, as evidenced by more downed branches. The breezes were warm though. He removed his mittens and overcoat. As Eb knew, Mother Nature often gave a false sense of relief from the harshness of winter. If he had not been so concerned about supplying his customers, he might have avoided the journey in January; traveling in the first month of the year was always taking a chance against a thaw. The sun's warming, once-welcome rays had persevered enough in the last several days to melt the packed snow to a boot-soaking slush in some sections and slippery, wet ice in shaded areas. Nip and Tuck were already straining with the new load, but the grip on the pung that the new, deep grooves created made it harder for them to drag the heavy sled through it. Ebenezer had tried to ease their burden by walking behind them. He slogged along, unable to avoid the icy sludge. His gelid toes felt like frozen sausages. The oxen stopped more than a few times when the slosh held tight to the runners on the pung or struck one of the many exposed rocks.

Travelers on the rough trails were always prepared for such hazards; what Ebenezer was not prepared for was a hazard directly affecting his body. His attention was directed ahead to a branch that had just fallen across the trail. Instead of waiting for the obstruction to bring Nip and Tuck to a halt, he turned to hop up quickly onto the pung to grab his axe. His left foot slipped and turned over on a slippery rock. The pain was stunning. Putting all his weight on his right foot precipitated a loss of balance. He involuntarily lunged to grab something on the pung that would keep him upright. The frantic "whoa" that he screeched resembled the cry of an animal in a sprung trap rather than a command directed at the steers. It took the team several seconds to respond, enough time for their master to lose his grip and spin to the right. He fell palms first. His hands slid along the granulated ice. It felt like saw blades.

"Damnation!" he shouted. Nip and Tuck must have mistaken the exclamation to mean "Keep on!" so they continued until reaching the obstruction ahead. Ebenezer was left on the ground to stare at his scraped hands, feel his ankle double in size, and sop up the frigid water with his trousers.

"Of all the totty-headed, stupid, goddamned animals!" he yelled at them. They had carried away the only support to help him stand. He surveyed the area to determine if there was anything useful to right himself. His ankle screamed for attention with the slightest twisting movement. He would have to attend to that first.

Movements he took for granted soon became an effort. He tried to keep his lower half still as he tugged at the stock around his neck to unwind it. Getting his foot out of his boot was the next struggle. He was able to accomplish this by holding his breath and giving a quick pull. He contorted his face and winced as his foot sent another angry message to his brain. Still sitting in an icy puddle, he wrapped his stock tightly around his foot and ankle and felt a modicum of relief. *Now, how to get up?*

His eye caught a fairly decent crutch-sized branch on the side of the trail. It was at the base of a pine not more than three body lengths away. He proceeded to drag and inch his way in its direction, fixing his eyes on it as though he were preventing it from getting up and running away.

His hands throbbed. He held his left hand up to dig his elbow into the icy mush as he used his good leg to drag his sopping body toward his target. His wet skin was beginning to burn from the cold.

He pulled the pine stick toward him and waited for a second for motivation to rise above the pain to hoist himself up. He was leaning on the stick and almost upright when he heard something up ahead.

The sound of a horse's snort and hooves that were anxiously dancing on the other side of the downed branch almost brought tears to his eyes. Horses and oxen stared at each other from opposite sides of the broken maple branch. Eb craned his head around a pine bough to try to make out the identity of the riders but was unable to see until he hobbled a few steps forward.

"Hey! Could ye help me? I've got myself in a bit of a pickle here!"

One of the riders studied Ebenezer for a second and, ignoring his request, said, "I believe we met on this road less 'n a fortnight ago. Ye must be comin' back from Salem, got yersef a nice loada rum, looks like," He was craning his head around to get a good look at Ebenezer's amassment of goods. He ran his tongue up his front teeth and made a sucking noise when he released it.

Ebenezer ignored the comment and pleaded, "I need some help gettin' up on my board, could ye—"

"Sure I ken help. Just that I'm very thirsty. This long ride has dried out my mouth, ye see." John Quigley looked to his brother, Willy, accompanied by an evil grin. Willy frowned hearing John's tone as though he were aware that it precipitated conflict. He turned in his saddle to face his younger brother more directly, narrowed his eyes, and cocked his head in warning. He uttered his name to caution him, "John?"

John disregarded the warning. He dismounted and

tied his horse to a birch sapling. Whatever John had in his mind, Ebenezer sensed this other man also suspected it was not congenial.

Willy, in contrast to his brother, respected the unspoken law of the land which typically expected a measure of assistance for those in need. Whether it came from a genuine concern or the knowledge that one day reciprocity might be required, the uncertain perils of the environment demanded interdependence. He approached the woeful figure.

"Steady, lean on me." Willy started to put Ebenezer's arm around his neck when he noticed the nasty scrapes on Mudgett's hands. "Wait a minute," he said, untying his neck handkerchief. "John, give me a hand here."

His brother was circling the pung with a hungry eye, like a bobcat ready to pounce on its prey.

"John! Lemme see yer stock," he shouted. "This man's got bloody hands!"

"A man with blood on his hands musta been up to nuthin' good!" he laughed.

"Seems like yer association with Whiting has rubbed offa ye. Now gimme yer stock." The perfunctory response finally had an effect.

Reluctantly, the younger Quigley strolled over and, unwrapping the soiled band from around his neck, threw it at his brother and walked back to the pung. Willy concentrated on wrapping Ebenezer's hands but was interrupted by a sudden thud. John had loosened the rope securing the top section of Mudgett's load. A barrel plummeted down, rolled a little, and stopped in front of an exposed rock.

Both Ebenezer and Willy were startled. If Eb had not sprained his ankle, he would have marched over to the reprehensible young man and given him a piece of his mind. He was limited to shouting out, "Whadja do that for?!"

"I need ta get myself a drink," John said, aware that Eb's injury would prevent any retaliation. He unplugged the cork. After hoisting the barrel waist high, he supported it on his thigh and circled his left arm around it like it was a girl to kiss. He heaved the barrel up over his head. The amber liquid started to pour out, but John couldn't maintain the cumbersome cask in the air for more than a few seconds. The rum soon missed its intended entrance and doused his face. Rivulets ran down his exposed neck and streamed between his cloak, waistcoat, and shirt before the barrel crashed onto the ground.

There was a loud crack, and the wooden bilge hoop gave way. Already weakened from the first fall, two of the barrel staves separated. The smell of rum floated in the air. The patches of snow that hadn't melted or frozen yet were absorbing the precious liquid as if something underneath were sucking it in.

"Aw, John, what's got into ye? Ye've been gettin' on my wick fer days now." This imperious attitude of John Quigley's was new. It had cropped up at the same time he was selected as Whiting's underling. It was as if the sheriff were contriving to mold him in his own likeness.

Willy turned to Ebenezer and gave a look of desperation and apology. He quickly tied the stock around Ebenezer's other hand. "Truly, sir, I'm sorry. Let me get ye to yer pung." He flashed an angry look at his younger brother who seemed to ignore the reprimand.

Eb demanded compensation for the rum. His authoritative voice fell on deaf ears. Willy had come to his aid, but his good nature did not extend to remuneration. He decided he was in no condition to pursue the matter any further.

John Quigley spat on the ground. He kicked some of the wooden stays out of his path and headed toward the obstruction. He shrugged as if to show that his brother had lost any influence over him. Ever since he had become Benjamin Whiting's deputy, he relished the chance to move out from under Willy's shadow and become *Deputy* Quigley instead of just *Willy's brother*. To ignore added recriminations, he turned his back and concentrated on removing the large branch.

Ebenezer leaned on Willy and the two ventured over to the pung. Every once in a while Eb winced as he put more pressure than was comfortable on his swollen ankle, but it was beginning to feel better with the wrapping. Willy managed to get Eb up on the board with the foot resting gently on the beam connecting Nip and Tuck.

"Ye'll be fine here fer a bit. Rest the foot," he said. "Ye've got 150 rods or thereabout before Jacob Paige's inn. Won't take ye more 'an fifteen minutes. They'll fix y'up." He turned around and cleared the remains of the barrel from the trail and then rebalanced the load on the pung. Ebenezer heard him cursing under his breath while tying the rope. He could feel the effect on the pung as Willy pulled tightly on the rope, uttering a condemnation of his brother's behavior with each tug.

Fortunately, it didn't take long to separate the branch blocking their paths into two manageable sections. Grunting, both brothers lifted up a section, pivoted it to a side, and heaved it out of the way with a loud thud.

Once the barrier was removed, the brothers and Ebenezer were free to go their separate ways. John mounted his mare and rode behind the pung to wait for his brother. Willy picked up the goad and walked his horse over to say farewell to Eb. He handed the whip to Ebenezer. The lacerations on his bound hands were not severe enough to prevent a good grip.

"Ye'll be fine, sir. Mr. Paige at the River Bend'll treat ye well. I, um, we wish ye a safe journey. God's speed." He mounted his horse. He touched the corner of his hat with two fingers to signal goodbye.

Eb urged the steers to move on. The pung glided well in some sections but not in others. Still, he maintained a decent pace and arrived at his destination without further issues. Ebenezer's trousers were still miserably wet, his hands throbbed, but his foot was only slightly uncomfortable now, as long as he didn't move it too much. The sign swinging in the wind for River Bend Inn was a wonderful sight.

The River Bend Inn

Ebenezer pulled up as close as possible to the inn and called to Jacob Paige for assistance. It took a few calls and several minutes, but the man finally appeared in the doorway. Jacob immediately recognized Ebenezer and hollered back.

"Afternoon, Mr. Mudgett. Ye got a fair load there. I expect ta ease yer rum burden a bit! Now, watcha hollerin' 'bout?" Jacob was wrapping his cloak around him as he strode over to see Eb.

"I encountered a problem back a ways. I need some help gettin' down and gettin' my team fixed up."

"Well, whatcha need first, Eb?" Jacob looked at the wrapped hands and foot and then at the anxious team. Nip and Tuck knew they were here to be fed and watered, and they were in no way going to stand still. Before he allowed Eb to respond, Jacob shouted in the direction of the barn for help.

"If ye could get Nip and Tuck here unhitched and settled in the barn first, I might be able ta get myself down. I don't dare try 'til they're separated. I need ta take it easy with this here foot."

Jacob released the cart beam and led the team over to the barn. Soon a handsome young man joined them. He nodded at Ebenezer and the older man sensed he was about the same age as his oldest son, Moses but a bit stronger and taller.

"This is my sister's boy, Ephraim. He's gonna help me out in the barn now. I'm not as young as I used to be! It's better that Ephraim's strong back lift the heavy stuff than my old spent one!"

Ebenezer, still sitting in his damp, cold pants, managed to smile for the first time in several hours and responded, "My boys have saved my ole back more 'an once, too. Good to meet ye, Ephraim."

Ephraim opened his mouth to say hello. The concentrated effort only produced a long series of the same syllable. His previously handsome face was contorted in what Ebenezer thought looked like agony while he desperately tried to force out the elusive word. *Should I help him say it?* Eb wondered. Finally, the last syllable emerged and Ephraim's face transformed back to its original, handsome contours. Unapologetic and turning to avoid further conversation, he directed his attention back to Nip and Tuck.

The oxen were eager to get to their reward. They quickly pushed into a large stall where the hay was already hanging from a net. Ephraim found a pole and entered the stall to break through a thin layer of ice in their bucket. If the two beasts had heard the sound of sloshing water, they ignored it. Instead they yanked out long strands of the dried grass. He gave each steer a pat on its rump and left to join Ebenezer and Jacob, who by now had managed to make it into the barroom and were standing close to the roaring fire.

The innkeeper was shaking his head in dismay while Eb filled him in on the recent events. As Ebenezer struggled to get his wet trousers off, Jacob's wife, Hannah, entered carrying a blanket under one arm while cupping her opposite hand over her eyes. Her presence did not interrupt Ebenezer's concentration, which was divided between telling his story and gingerly sliding his pant leg over the injured ankle.

"I know the Quigley brothers well, and though I'm not surprised at John's behavior, I'm disappointed to hear it," Jacob sighed.

Still listening, Jacob found a pail and put a few hot coals in the bottom. He rested a narrow board on top and when Eb sat down, he instructed him to put his foot on top. The warmth rising from the coals felt good on his foot.

"Well, I guess luck shone down on ye that Willy was with him. It wasn't that long ago they'd both be in here and John'd look at Willy like he was a king. He wouldn't do or say anythin' without lookin' at Willy first and last," he said. Jacob lowered his head slightly and smiled in remembrance. Suddenly he lifted his head up and said, "I blame that Whiting. Seems like John Quigley changed after gettin' that position. It's gone to his head. Last time he was here he picked a fight with Ephraim."

Ebenezer noticed the embarrassed look on Ephraim's face. The strapping young man did not look as if he desired to relive that event.

"Quigley narrowed in on Ephraim's stammer and, like an animal going after wounded prey, wouldn't stop with his insults. Ephraim could have easily overwhelmed him. He's a head taller and carries more heft to him," Jacob said. "Ephraim was gettin' ready to lunge at him, but I held him back. Had he succeeded, Benjamin Whiting would surely have intervened soon after—and it would not have been in Ephraim's favor."

They were interrupted by two men storming into the inn, laughing and shouting. One was carrying a sack, swinging it back and forth. He stopped in the middle of the room, one hand on his hip and his feet spread for balance. When he noticed he was the center of attention, he reached into the sack and pulled out a whole cooked cow's tongue, holding it high above his head.

"There is a tongue that never told a lie, and I doubt there is another such in the room!"

In unison, the small group burst into laughter. Even Ebenezer relaxed in his chair and released the first hearty laugh he had had in a week. He let the wave of jocularity engulf him like a soft cloud. The pleasure of the moment was due in part to the rum toddy Jacob's hefty wife had brought him. He made a decision to let go of the week's tribulations and allow the congeniality and comfort of the inn to wrap around him like a warm blanket.

"Hannah, get a look at Ebenezer's hands. He needs some attention," Jacob whispered to his wife. It wouldn't be the first time she would have to administer palliative care, nor the last.

Ebenezer didn't want to let go of his heavenly libation, but Hannah, used to dealing with stubborn men, gave him a look that made anything less than compliance out of the question. He swiftly gulped as much of the warm liquid as he could, set the vessel down, and raised his hands as if offering her a gift. She gently unwound the handkerchiefs. Ebenezer winced softly when she had to pull at the cloth adhered to his wounds. He was happy to discover his hands weren't badly swollen.

"Ayup, they look sore, but not too serious. I'll get ye a basin of water and some cloth. I might even have some wild daisy mixed with hog fat ta ease the burnin'. Ye'll be back ta yer ole self!" Hannah's neck had long disappeared, replaced by a pillow of flesh that jiggled whenever she spoke. Coupled with her jovial smile, it gave her a jolliness. Somehow it all translated into comforting Ebenezer, and he couldn't help but smile at her in return, or perhaps it was the grog finding its way to his brain.

The affable man with the cow's tongue was still commanding the center of attention. Jacob's customers slid their chairs to face him. They wore the kind of expectant expressions born from those who knew to anticipate more of his antics. They began encouraging him to tell some of his wild tales for the benefit of those who did not know him, or because they enjoyed hearing the exaggerations again themselves. Topics were being loudly suggested from various parts of the room. The man, who didn't need the prodding, placed his supper on the table and pulled out a chair. Still standing, he put one foot up on it and leaned in on his bent leg. After cutting a big wedge of the meat, he stabbed it with his knife, and took a big bite. He began telling his story in between chewing and piercing more of the gelatinous, pink chunks. Ebenezer smiled and laughed with the rest of them, even though some of the words were unintelligible and muffled by the mouthfuls. The pure pleasure he felt rising deep inside him from the warmth, the conviviality, and the rum made anything the man said seem funny, whether he understood him or not. Hannah returned with strips from an old sheet and a tin with a greasy concoction. She spread it on Ebenezer's palms and rewrapped his hands. He barely noticed.

Jacob Paige's inn was more comfortable than most. The beds, piled with quilts made by Hannah's hand over the years, were stuffed with goose feathers, and the sheets were usually clean. If the inn had been busy, he would have had to share the bed with another traveler; however, this night the bed was all his, not that he noticed. He had fallen into a drunken stupor and Ephraim had half-carried him and deposited him on the bed.

Ebenezer sunk into a deep slumber. He was mumbling in between fits of resounding snores. The next morning he would forget the disconcerting dream with the likes of the Salem man, Quigley, Whiting, and Sherburn popping in and out to haunt him. At times they worked in unison, contriving to put obstacles in his way to prevent him from returning home. Other times they teamed up to denigrate him for abusing the Pine Tree Law and defying the Crown. He began to stir when his dream turned to images of his children hiding behind the logs at Clement's sawmill.

The hustle and bustle downstairs woke him with a start. He quickly sat up and peeled his sweaty shirt from his back. Someone had closed the curtains, but the slice of light between the fabric and the window frame told him it was late. He had hoped to rise before the sun to make it home today. He pushed and kneed the quilts out of the way with his good foot and swung his legs gingerly over the side so he could sit.

He made a swift assessment of his condition. He slowly stretched out his hands and then made fists, noting improvement. The hog fat Hannah had slathered on his palms had seeped into the fabric strips of cloth, and traces of it had smeared onto the sheets and his shirt. He unwound the cloth and studied his hands. *Not bad*, he thought, *though still tender.* He then directed his attention to his foot; he attempted to slowly wiggle it and determined that it had improved, but he would still have to favor it. The swelling had lessened. After rewrapping his foot, he looked around for his boots. Someone had placed both by a wooden chair near the bed. He was sure he had forgotten the left one on his pung. He smiled.

"M-m-m-m-mornin' Mr. M-m-m-udgett," Ephraim greeted him as he entered the dining room. "H-h-how are ye to-to-today?"

"The head is wishin' I took it easier last night, but the body seems improved," he said, rubbing his temples. He noticed Ephraim had a sturdy pole with a piece of linen wrapped around the short crosspiece at the top.

"I-I-I made ye a cr-cr-crutch." He said and handed it to Ebenezer, who smiled in return.

"That'll do just fine!" Eb said, shoving it under his arm pit. He took a few steps, grasping it more with his arm than his hand, and nodded his approval.

Ebenezer saw Jacob in the opposite doorway. "Looks like Ephraim got the height just right."

"Nice handiwork, Ephraim. I thank ye!"

The young man didn't respond but tilted his head, smiled, and nodded.

Ebenezer and Jacob walked to the desk to settle up. Ebenezer had delivered enough rum to cover the cost of the room and board for a night and then some. After Jacob paid Eb for the difference and finished ribbing him about the night's frivolity, he announced, "Ephraim got yer team all hitched and ready. He tied 'em to the rail and threw 'em a little hay to keep 'em occupied. How're ye feelin' now?

"Not as bad as yesterday nor as good as the morrow, but fine enough," he said, hobbling around.

Ephraim turned to leave, but Hannah barreled

passed him. She almost pushed him over with her wide hips. Her little feet were shuffling in a quick step as she called Ebenezer's name.

"Oh good, I thought I had missed ye, Mr. Mudgett. Here take these bannocks. I just got 'em outta the oven. I put some jam in a tin fer ye." She handed a small cloth sack to her husband and Eb inhaled the aroma of the warm oatmeal cakes.

"Ah, Mistress Paige, I would not dare tell my wife, but ye make the best bannocks of any woman I know!"

Hannah stood with her hands on her ample hips and a pleased expression crossed her face. It wasn't the first time she had been praised for her baking. "Aaw, Mr. Mudgett!"

"I guess ye owe me 'nother barrel of rum now!" Jacob laughed.

The three men walked slowly outside to where Ephraim had hitched the team to a post. The temperature had dipped considerably from the previous days and Eb was greeted by a gust of icy wind. He pushed his chin down into his muffler and bore the blast with an air of defiance. Ephraim helped him up onto the board and Jacob handed him the sack. Eb thanked them profusely and started on the last leg of his journey.

The Homecoming

Eb had a lot to mull over; the days alone on the trail provided ample opportunity and not being able to run to keep warm, he occupied his mind with his problems.

Ebenezer stopped at two more taverns along the way; he arrived at each hunched over and shivering. The roaring fires thawed him out, and he sipped enthusiastically on the warmed grog. Ebenezer was eager to share the story of the growing dissidence permeating the cities and towns of Massachusetts, but he had to be cautious. Spies were known to frequent the taverns; therefore, he could only share his report when he was familiar with the clientele and their political sensitivities. Once Eb was sure that the environment did not harbor sympathies toward England, he revealed the conversation with the gentleman in Salem and the implication that resistance was growing. He shared *the Massachusetts Spy* to inspire the settlers to share their own experiences.

In the first tavern, the men were reticent to divulge any incidents concerning the King's White Pine Law or his appointed officials. However, Eb could tell they were empathetic by the head-bobbing and grunts in the right places. In the second tavern, the men were more vocal and offered experiences of their own. It seemed that all sawmills in the area held unlawful timber. The timber owners' anger against the greedy King and men like Sherburn, Quigley, and Whiting was stronger than their guilt for having defied the law. The topic of what to do brought heated discussion on both sides, even though the general opinions toward England mirrored those of his own: They had to cut ties with the overbearing mother. The sole contention was *how* to do it. *At least*, he thought, *I have provided the New Hampshire people with a fair perspective on the developing activities beyond New Hampshire's border.* He was laying the groundwork.

Ebenezer was but fifty rods from receiving a grand homecoming when he ran into Timothy Worthley, riding home from his brother Jonathan's home. Eb was still anxious to share his concerns; however, he was more eager to plant a kiss on Miriam's cheek.

"Hey, neighbor! Did ye lose the rest of yer party?" Timothy teased.

"They'll be showin' up in a day or so. Caleb was workin' to get ye a fine price for yer leathers." The customary strength and richness in his voice sounded strangely subdued.

"Are you feelin' well? It looks like ye met with a

bear on the trail." Timothy acknowledged the crutch with an upper flick of his chin.

"Ye could say that and not lie," Ebenezer said. "I'd like ye to help me spread the word; we need to have a meetin'. I want to wait fer the rest of 'em to come back, and I have to handle some business at the sawmill but, say, a week from today at my house?"

"Sure, friend. I can let it be known. Sounds direful. What do ye want me to say?"

"Just say, *justice*." Eb quickly snapped the goad to avoid further discussion. He didn't want to say more to have the message twisted and turned as it circulated the Weare villages. He wanted his neighbors and friends to hear *his* carefully planned words and not the distorted ones. He left Timothy scratching his head.

It was a welcome sight to see the smoke rising from his chimney twirling and twisting as if beckoning him home. The oxen didn't need any encouragement to move faster. As he approached the house and barn, he gave his best rendition of an Indian holler. Excited faces appeared in the window, their mouths moving, shouting unintelligible greetings. Soon the youngest ones crowded in the doorway jumping out of sync and waving frantically. He laughed and waved back.

"Papa didn't forget! I have some sweets!" he shouted.

He had said the magic word; the youngest children spontaneously bounded out of the house and ran in his direction. The arctic gusts tried to push them back, but their excitement to see their father and discover what delights he had brought were no match for winter winds.

"Children! Come fetch yer cloaks!" Miriam stood on the first granite step holding baby John, just as Ebenezer had seen her weeks before. The children were impervious to her plea, as Miriam's grin showed she knew they would be, and they ran after their father. Their giggles and squeals filled the space between them. She hoped their excitement would override the desire to inform their father about their unwanted visitor.

Miriam retreated inside to wait for the children to come dashing back. She had tears in her eyes as she busied herself stoking the fire. Since Whiting's visit, she had peered out the window more times than she could count. Her relief in finally detecting the familiar team of oxen and the hunched figure driving them had released a wave of unexpected emotion. She quickly dabbed her eyes with her apron and joined Ezra at the window. She smiled at his attempt to conceal his anticipation; it wasn't long ago that he acted just as giddy as his siblings. As he approached manhood, he had been conscious not to display the same emotions he disdained in the younger ones. Miriam put her arm around Ezra and tilted her head until it touched his. He tolerated the affection.

Sarah couldn't wait any longer. She bolted out of the house, trying to wrap her cloak around her as she ran. Her arms encircled her father's neck, nearly knocking him backward. Her height closely matched his now. "Did ye get me the ribbons, father?"

"How could I forget ye!" He laughed.

Enveloped in the winter cold, the children ran back into the house, each carrying a prized possession, and sat near the warmth of the fire. Eb stumbled inside as if pushed by a blast of cold air, looking more like a vagabond than the dignified man that had departed a fortnight ago. He wrapped his arms around Ezra and gave him a bear hug while smiling at Miriam standing behind him. Once again, the tears welled up in her eyes. Ebenezer was surprised; she rarely showed such sentiment.

"Get yer coat on, son, and help Moses with the steers and the unloadin'. I'll be out there directly." The limp in his step when he released Ezra concerned Miriam.

"It appears yer journey may not have been without some difficulty, Ebenezer," she frowned, studying her husband from top to toe.

"Just a minor inconvenience, dear. Ye can see I'm all in one piece!" He was glad that his mittens hid the evidence of further injury, if just for the time being. He hobbled a step before she managed to reach him and to give him the hug she longed for during his absence.

"I expected ye before this, old man! The weather wasn't so bad as to take up the full two weeks," she said suddenly pulling away and wiping the tear that had rolled down her cheek. "I thought a wildcat had ye fer supper!"

"Just about, Miriam, just about."

Later that night, as baby John was finally lulled to

sleep and the children were quiet, they had their opportunity to speak freely. With some difficulty negotiating the stairs, Ebenezer followed Miriam into the root cellar, their usual haven to talk freely without concern of being overheard. He sensed there was a story behind his wife's tears, and he feared Sheriff Whiting might have something to do with them. As soon as Miriam planted her feet on the dirt floor, she faced her husband, one step above, and said, "We had a visitor a few days ago, husband." She paused and then couldn't help but add, "Did ye by any chance do *anything* on the road to provoke the county *sheriff?*"

Ebenezer took the last step slowly as though his wife's words had made all his muscles seize up. He rested his wrists on his wife's shoulders and stared into her eyes. The serious look in his eyes answered her question.

"Did he come here?" he demanded. "Did he vex ye or the children?"

Miriam spared no detail. Ebenezer listened intently while clenching his teeth. His finger drew circles in the dust on a jar as she spoke, but the finger paused when she mentioned the disturbing scrutiny Whiting gave Sarah. When she finished, he looked into her eyes.

"He came to intimidate me through you. He just wanted to frighten ye enough so ye'd be forwardin' his implied admonition directly to me." He hugged her close and whispered, "It's all right, Miriam. *I didn't hurt his person* as he said. To be honest, I wanted to, but I didn't."

He held her for a minute longer and sighed deeply. It was his turn to share. The locked door in his soul, where he harbored the causes of all the built-up anxiety, burst open. His despair and frustration spilled out. He explained how he defied the Pine Tree Law. He told of the consequences, and his interactions with Sheriff Whiting, his deputy, John Quigley, and Governor Wentworth's deputy, John Sherburn. After unburdening himself, he inhaled slowly. He then revealed the Salem stranger's implicit call to resist authority.

"I served Weare as a constable back in 1768, for God's sake! I have always lived my life by the same rules I endeavor to instill in our children: Be honest, work hard, and obey the laws! My unhappy situation has obliged me to fall away from the law, wife," he moaned, striking his balled fist against his forehead. "I have little option but to continue on this road and to call for others to join me. This law is unjust! We have no legal means to pursue our disfavor of it; we must take a stand. Still, it tears at my gut!"

It was Miriam's turn to rest her hand on his shoulder. As concerned as she was with the revelations, she whispered, "At last I am hearing the truth." Ebenezer gave her a puzzled look.

"For months now, I have fretted that ye have kept something from me. Ye always said yer worries were none enough to burden me. But they were sufficient to creep into yer dreams at night and cause ye to mutter in yer sleep. They even haunted ye in the day makin' ye argue with yerself in a rough fashion. I know ye well, husband. Ye will make the right decision on how to handle this."

"That is my perplexity!" he said, harsher than he wanted, "There is no *right* to this wrong!"

The Reckoning

The next day the sun was shyly peering over the trees and well beyond the Kuncanoet Hills in the east, but the cheerfulness of the sun's rays would have little impact on the darkness ahead. This day in the winter of 1772 would test Ebenezer's nerves and finally bring to fruition what he had been fearing in his heart. After a restless sleep, he had risen early and made his way to Clement's sawmill.

Ebenezer knew that Sherburn would turn up soon. Their confrontation at the Goat's Head Inn was likely to have instilled a need for vengeance on Sherburn's part. His masculinity had been challenged in front of his friends. No better way to retaliate than for the governor's deputy to catch some pines in the sawmill with the King's Broad Arrow—or pines that had the broad arrow mark hacked out of them.

Knowing that he was not alone in the contravention did little to ease his mind; in fact, it made it worse. What nagged him the most was the knowledge that his pines were not the only ones resting at the sawmill. It didn't set well with him to know that his friends and neighbors with less means were in jeopardy. He had made his choice for his logs and would have to live with the consequences, but he was uncomfortable with them assuming the risk as well.

It was impossible to ignore the logs yet to be sawed; they were laying in stacks everywhere. Ebenezer urged the log-cutters to keep up the pace before someone showed up to inspect the sawmill. *One log at a time*, he thought—the mantra that played over and over in his mind. The conundrum was that a few of the pines were so massive it would take days to reduce them to anywhere near a size that would betray their original state. Ebenezer reflected on the story he had heard when people first settled in the town. Some of the pines were cut seventeen rods long, and their stumps were so broad that a yoke of oxen could easily mount and turn around on them. The pines in Clement's sawmill were not that gigantic, but a significant number of them had dwarfed the other trees in the forests, and by law, belonged to the King.

There was a lull in the screeching of the two-man saw blade when he heard the snow crunching under impatient hooves. He turned to see a familiar, cloaked figure staring down at him. The rider had a very unpleasant countenance, an evil smile as if to relish Mudgett's look of surprise. Behind the rider were two mounted men. Suddenly, Ebenezer's stomach contracted into a hard stone.

"Ah, Mr. Mudgett! A pleasure to see ye again, sir!" Sherburn's voice spiked to an uncomfortable level. To make up for this, he straightened in his saddle, cleared his throat and continued. He managed to lower his voice and speak officiously, "I am here for the pleasure of the King as deputy to the Surveyor of the King's Wood. I am to inspect and record the trees on this property." Without waiting for a response, he dismounted and tied his steed to the nearest post. The other men followed suit, the leathers squeaking with the shift in weight as the men slid off their horses.

Eb registered again that Sherburn was a good deal shorter than he was, although this advantage wouldn't serve him any real purpose. Nothing would serve him well at this point, except a miracle whereby the timber would simply disappear. There was no hiding the ignominious fact that Mudgett and his friends had defied the King's order and would have to pay the consequences. He only wished he could calm the rapid beating of his heart and swallow away the dry knot in his throat. Despite the inner workings of his body, Mudgett portrayed a very calm exterior. He simply gave a quick nod to the man as if he were allowed to grant permission for this invasion.

The inspection was short, limited to a mere glance around the sawmill. Sherburn directed little snorts of triumph toward each stack. The measure of the infraction would be of little consequence; it would only take one log to be considered defiant, and there were hundreds of them. The other men scattered to the various piles to count the offending timber. A pudgy man, red-faced by the cold and excited by his discovery, jogged over to Sherburn and announced his tally.

"270 logs!"

"Sir, there appears to be a good deal of large timber fit for masts for the Royal Navy," he appeared delighted to announce. "I do not need ta tell ye and the owners of the timber that ye've disobeyed the edict," he sniffed. "Ye know to look in the *New Hampshire Gazette* for the day and time to appear in court. The contraband will be confiscated fer King George. I'll get the names of the owners so fines can be paid."

Ebenezer believed the short man had grown a few inches. He, on the other hand, felt quite small. Ebenezer had lost the race against time. He had nothing to say; nothing he could say anyway. The evidence stacked all around him had silenced his authoritative voice.

Even if he could muster the energy to speak, he would have been interrupted by the shout sailing through the cold air from one of the men standing in front of Ebenezer's stack of pines. All of the logs had distinguishing cuts and hacks to hide the royal mark. The King's servants were laughing at the prospect that someone believed expunging the broad arrows would disguise the massive pines. Ebenezer exhaled a long sigh and endured the humiliation.

On February 5, 1772, the *New Hampshire Gazette* published the citation. Whether the accused had taken the word seriously about the meeting or not, the published citation, Ebenezer knew, would convince them to come. He grabbed his copy of the *Gazette* and headed to Quimby's Inn. When Eb entered, he recognized only a few of the travelers presently engaged in raucous conversations. He was pleased to notice Timothy Worthley and Abraham Johnson.

"Friends, I've got a paper here t'will make fer some more interestin' conversation than ye've been havin'," he interrupted, his voice a bit louder than usual to be sure he had their attention. "Will ye allow me to read it fer ye?" Ebenezer wasted no time waiting for a response.

> *"All persons claiming property in the following WHITE PINE LOGS, seized by order of the SURVEYOR GENERAL in Goffstown and Weare, in the Province of New Hampshire, may appear at Court of Vice Admiralty to be held at Portsmouth, on Thursday the 27th instant at Ten of the clock a.m. and shew cause why the same should not be declared forfeited, agreeable to all information filed in said Court."*

Timothy and Abraham exchanged nervous glances. They had expected the citation, but hearing the formality of it registered deeper. Abraham pulled on his beard while Ebenezer read the offending sawmills. Timothy stared at his boots and swiped at the lock of hair that fell across his face.

> *"200 White Pine Logs from 15 or 30 inches diameter lying at Richard's mill in*
> *Goffstown*
> *250 Ditto from 15 to 13 inches diameter at Patty's mill.*
> *35 Ditto from 36 to 20 ditto at Dow's mill.*
> *140 Ditto from 30 to 18 ditto at Asa Patty's old mill."*

Here Ebenezer paused and cleared his throat. He peered over the top of the paper, meeting the eyes of all the men in the room, and then focusing on Timothy and Abraham, he announced, "270 Ditto from 36 to 17 ditto at Clement's Mill in Weare."

"So there we have it." Abraham rested his hands on his ample belly. He didn't need to hear any more. Ebenezer walked over to his friends while exchanges sprung up among the different groups.

"What is our recourse now, friend?" Timothy asked.

"We are obliged to go on the 27th to defend ourselves. Did ye not hear the man?" Abraham said, poking Timothy with his elbow. He took the paper from Ebenezer and read the last lines to himself, then said, "He wasted no time, now did he? John Sherburn signed it February 5th, the wee weasel. It appears that Clement's sawmill was one of the last stops, his crownin' glory, it was."

"I'll take the south road to meet with and encourage our friends to show up tomorrow night. You both cover the rest. I don't know what the other sawmills in Weare and the other towns are plannin' to do, but it wouldn't hurt to ask around," Ebenezer stated. "I fer one will be damned if I will pay a shilling to the King."

Representation

*E*benezer alternated pacing the meeting room floor at his house and poking at the logs in the fire. He anticipated all seven of his friends showing up to discuss the action, or perhaps the inaction, he and the other offenders should take. Caleb Atwood and William Dustin had arrived an hour early to get a tankard of rum into their bellies before the meeting.

"Serious talk always goes down easier accompanied with some rum!" William announced. The two sat down where they would have easy access to the reactions of all present. They both contemplated the concern showing on Ebenezer's face.

Caleb attempted to lighten the tension and hopefully erase the frown etched in Mudgett's brow. "It is told," he began with an impish smile on his face, "that John Hodgdon has been buyin' up more land in a score of towns. Why just the other night, two young people were out lookin' up at the moon and discussin' if there was land on the dark parts. Polly Tuttle said she'd go and ask John Hodgdon. *He'll know*, she said. *If it is land, he has got a mortgage on it!*" William responded with a hoot. They both looked over at Ebenezer who was rubbing the stubble on his chin and staring into the fire. He hadn't moved. One outstretched arm was rigid with his hand gripping the mantel, the other hand resting in his pocket.

Caleb tried again to get a rise out of Ebenezer. "I swear that John Hodgdon's dish is always right side up whenever it rains porridge." William laughed and looked at Ebenezer. This time Ebenezer turned to face them and nodded. A slight smile eased his frown, but it soon disappeared. His troublesome thoughts swallowed him up again.

Jesse, little Miriam, and William, curious about the sudden gaiety of the conversation, peered into the room. They were about to enter, but their mother caught them and herded them back toward the kitchen. Ezra and Moses took advantage of her distraction and slipped into the meeting room. Their father's natural good humor had been scarce since his return; even Sarah had mentioned it. They wanted to know why. The promise of a thick wedge of johnnycake fresh from the open fire and dripping with maple syrup was not going to tempt them back to the kitchen.

Within minutes of each other, Timothy and Jonathan Worthley, Abraham Johnson, Jotham Tuttle, and Will Quimby, the innkeeper's brother, crossed the threshold. The citation had named them in the *Gazette*, along with Ebenezer, Caleb, and William Dustin.

Ebenezer waited for them to get settled and was about to begin when suddenly young Samuel Goodale stumbled in. He stood in the doorway, as though unsure if he would be welcome in the closed assembly.

"Samuel! Ye are as innocent in this citation as Moses and Ezra there hidin' in the back!" Jotham said. "Have ye come to help, hinder, or hoot?"

"I figure that had I been able, my logs'd be there right with yers. Maybe I ken help in some fashion."

The men grinned, and Caleb raised his tankard, "Give the fella a toddy and let's get this over with. My wife needs me to warm the bed soon!"

"As ye all know only too well," Ebenezer began, "we have been cited to come to Portsmouth to show cause why we should not forfeit our trees and pay the fine."

"And—as ye all know," Abraham interrupted, "King George himself will pardon us and send us back with extra shillings in our pockets fer our trouble!" The men groaned, snickered, or humphed.

Ebenezer raised his hand to silence the grumblings. "As I've stated before, I will not pay another shilling for *my* pine trees I bought on *my* land, then again paid a license merely to look at them! I object having to give them *happily* over to the Crown. A *fig* fer the law!"

"T'is true we do not *want* to, but I don't see, friend, how we can avoid it. England has tied our hands in this matter," Will Quimby offered, running his fingers through his beard.

"I fer one, do not see why we have been summoned to Portsmouth to plead fer a cause that has already been determined. We have been away from our families long enough, havin' just returned from Salem." Caleb said, "I do not relish a long journey to and fro just to get myself told I'm to be fined. My wife has slept in a cold bed long enough!"

"Do we just sit and wait fer Whiting to round us up then?" Abraham asked.

Samuel had been following the conversation from the back of the room and was bobbing his head in agreement with everyone who had spoken. He suddenly stood and addressed the room.

"Why not send someone in yer place?" "T'is certain the journey would be a wasted one. Why not allow another to waste his time instead of ye. Between the eight of ye, the cost would not be too dear."

"The boy is right," William Dustin smiled, "We need someone to represent us."

The other men, appreciating Samuel's logic, uttered words of agreement.

"Who should we send?" Jotham asked.

"I'll ask Sam Blodgett from Goffstown. He has handled some business with me before and goes into Portsmouth regularly. He's a dodgy sort but a good talker. He can talk the stinger out of a bee. I trust it would be a small hardship fer him to manage this task," Ebenezer said.

"Are ye sure he'll represent us offenders? After all, we're accused of takin' the *King's* property, not some ole settler's in the woods," Jonathan Worthley said. Timothy supported his brother with a nod.

"Sam Blodgett is well known for followin' the scent of a coin or two. If we pay him enough, he will do our bidding. With the prospect of more coins in his pocket, he ken be very cunning." Ebenezer added, "He might even sweet talk our way out of this mess."

Caleb stood up, "Sounds like he's the man to do the job!"

"It's settled then," Abraham said. "Now, let us shake this unpleasantness off with a rum toddy fit for King George himself!" The others raised no objections, and the mood in the room improved considerably.

Ebenezer went to each sawmill charged in the citation and collected enough currency to entice Blodgett to represent them and argue on their behalf. As Ebenezer expected, Sam Blodgett was due to journey into Portsmouth and welcomed the opportunity to increase his earnings on the same trip. In fact, the avaricious man had snatched the leather pouch out of Ebenezer's hands before Eb had a chance to strengthen his plea with his prepared testimony. Ebenezer hoped Sam Blodgett's greediness was an indication that he would endeavor to deliberate well on their behalf. Lately, he had heard rumors that Blodgett had a tendency to lean toward the wind blowing in the most favorable direction, yet Eb had been favorably impressed with how the pudgy little man conducted himself when Eb needed help in his business. He studied the man currently peering into the leather pouch, ascertaining if enough coins represented his ability as an advocate. He was better dressed than when they last met: silk breeches and waistcoat, a lacy cravat around his neck, clean white leggings, and a scarlet knee-length frock. He wore a wig with tight curls covering his ears, and his beaver felt three-cornered hat sat on his desk, ready to carry; it wouldn't fit over his wig. Ebenezer thought to himself, *his undeniable success surely must be a good sign.*

On February 11, 1772, six days after the citation appeared, Samuel Blodgett secured an audience with Governor John Wentworth. Blodgett's timing turned out to be very convenient for the chief of state, who had recently decided that he needed to hire someone to monitor John Sherburn as deputy to the Surveyor of the King's Woods. He had received too many complaints about the deputy's behavior. As Wentworth listened intently to Blodgett, the governor was evaluating not only the petitioner's power of persuasion but his comportment as well. He concluded that the man before him would be a more tactful deputy than the hot-headed Sherburn.

They discussed a settlement for the mills in the Piscataquog Valley towns: The men would have to pay a certain amount, the logs would be given up to them, and the cases would be dropped. When Samuel Blodgett walked out of the meeting, he was smiling. Without even trying, he had secured a prominent position for himself with a large territory and the promise of generous compensation. The governor was also smiling; he had been pleasantly surprised at how easy it was to manipulate the man into violating his friends' trust.

Blodgett's first duty was to inform the particular offenders, those whom he had betrayed, that the governor was not going to yield his position against the miscreants, but had lightened the penalty. He could not do this without revealing he had switched sympathies and been rewarded for it. His delight after taking the governor's leave was tinged with a sinking feeling as to how he would bring this new information to light. He delayed communicating the news for two weeks, until February 24th. He took the option any good coward would take: writing a letter rather than confronting the wounded parties.

Resistance Brews

The children surrounded their father. Ebenezer had piled the long oak table with the horses' tack to teach them the importance of cleaning and preserving the leather. William would be inheriting the task from Ezra, who had graduated into more strenuous chores. Jesse was curious and was playing with the metal bits and reins. He glanced at his sister Miriam. The impish look on his face revealed he had designs to attach the contraption to her somehow and ride her around the house.

"Boys have all the good chores," Sarah lamented.

The rapid knocks pecking at the front door sounded like a woodpecker's search for insects.

Miriam and Claire were occupied in the kitchen cutting up root vegetables for the stew. Miriam glanced at Claire, a look that was sufficient to convince the housemaid to answer the impatient knocks on the door.

The lesson with his children and the visitor

knocking at the door divided Ebenezer's attention, but he continued talking. He grabbed the reins out of Jesse's hands. Jesse reacted by emitting a mournful howl. His father suspected he had envisioned great fun at the expense of his sister.

"Mr. Mudgett, there is a letter fer ye, sir," Claire said with her hand outstretched.

"A letter, Papa! Who's it from?" Ezra marveled. The children stood with mouths open, expecting wondrous things to be revealed from inside the envelope. They watched as he broke the seal and opened the missive. He had been expecting something from Portsmouth. This letter certainly was it. He stood perfectly still, gripping the paper; not a muscle moved except his eyes which darted back and forth across it. The children peppered him with questions, but he ignored them.

"Miriam!" he shouted. "Children, wait here. I'll be back in a minute." Ebenezer ran off with the crumpled letter clenched high and his lips pursed in fierce determination. Jesse smiled, reached for the reins, and studied his sister Miriam with glee.

Eb found his wife bending down, gently putting the baby in his cradle. Ebenezer's mind veered from the vexing letter to thinking John was getting too big for his bed, but by the time Miriam stood to face him, the thought washed from his mind. She cocked her head as he showed her the letter. She was about to take it and read for herself, but he shook it in the air, "That blasted mealymouthed . . . chuckle-headed . . . !" Miriam put a hand on his shoulder and gently guided him outside the room, away from the sleeping baby.

"The unctuous scalawag!" he hissed through tight lips. Seeing he was incapable of summarizing the letter, she took it from him. She clutched it with both hands and read:

"The late seizure of White pine Logs, has caused me a disagreeable journey to Portsmouth, at the special request of a number of my friends, to solicit the governor in behalf of them who have necessarily trespassed in cutting the King's timber." Her hand was shaking. She cleared her throat and continued, *"His excellency thought fit to deputise me one of his Majesty's Surveyors of the King's woods in this Western District, thereby authorizing me to carry the King's laws into execution. As they are very severe, I shall be loth to prosecute, unless obstinate or notorious offenders force it upon me; of which I give you this early notice, at the same time acquaint you his Excellency has pleased to put it in my hands to make the matter easy to you. Sam Blodgett."*

"*Loathe* to do so, humph!" Miriam added, "What are ye plannin' to do, husband?"

"He wrote to all of us. Certainly, the others will be just as chafed and will appear on our doorstep on the morrow." He took the letter from her. "Obstinate and notorious offenders are we! I can tell ye surely; *we* are not the notorious offenders!" *Our heads won't be settling much on our pillows tonight,* he thought.

Ebenezer's prediction came to pass. He was wide awake after tossing and turning for an hour. Eb knew he would not be able to fall asleep. Miriam was snoring, won over by a deep slumber. The shifting quilts and squeaking wood frame stopped the snoring momentarily, and he waited for it to resume before slipping out of bed. Ebenezer crept downstairs and headed for the fireplace. He found the long iron hook to stir the glowing embers. He coaxed them into producing flames and then rolled the charred back-log to the front and watched it catch fire. Eb became mesmerized by the dancing and flickering flames licking the smoky air. After a short while, as his thoughts took precedence over the blazing spectacle, Ebenezer resorted to the position he often took when needing to solve problems. He stretched his right arm out straight, pushed against the mantel, and shifted his weight onto his left leg, his right one bent. With his head down, Eb was able to clear his thoughts and concentrate. He needed to think what he would say to his friends. Ebenezer remained in the same position for ten minutes before he switched legs. When he did, he knew what he was going to say to the men.

Like mercury absorbing bits of itself, the men collected each other and arrived at Mudgett's house mid-morning, just as he knew they would. Not all brought their letters, but all brought foul moods.

"The wretch!" Will Quimby said. "He was supposed to represent us. How dare he now represent the governor!"

"He can make it *easy* fer us, he wrote," Jotham grimaced.

"Not *fer* us, just because it's him and not someone else demandin' we pay up. How generous of him!" Abraham sniggered.

"The turncoat!" Jonathan Worthley began, "How . . . ?"

"We know *how*. The silver stacked in front of him swayed him!" his brother Timothy interrupted.

"Maybe we should have emptied our pockets more," Caleb offered, his cheeks burning with anger.

"No, we knew at the start we were in a pickle." During the sleepless night, Ebenezer had become circumspect, and he exuded the same prudence in the meeting. His calm reserve was beginning to soothe his compatriots.

"We wanted to trust that he could say something to get us out of it. I'm not sayin' he isn't churlish for turning on us, but the fact is, our gripe is not with Blodgett, it's with who it always has been: the governor and the King."

"Ebenezer is right," William Dustin piped up, "The son of a sow is just the governor's abettor. What we need to do is plan our course of action."

They all looked to Ebenezer. He drew a breath, crossed his arms, and said, "*No* action."

"What?" they said in unison. They exchanged astonished looks.

"We are going to resist! No action is indeed action; it is agitation. We must go to all the other sawmills and tell them to refuse to pay," he responded.

"Eb, you can't be serious. They'll haul us off and chuck us in jail!" William Dustin said, looking around the room at his friends. His boney hands fluttered slightly by his sides.

"If we pay," Ebenezer stated, "the outrage will continue, and we will never get rid of this Pine Tree Law. Don't ye want the pines for yourselves? The opportunity is now! Not only for ourselves . . . but for our children! We can not allow this indignity to continue. It is time we stood up and made our enmity clear. They did it in Massachusetts. They even did it in Portsmouth when they burned George Meserve, the postmaster, in effigy! We can do it in Weare!

Jotham stood up. "I fer one am weary of bein' indebted to anyone, especially the Crown. Our fathers and grandfathers came across the ocean to be free. I don't feel free with the almighty King tellin' me what I can and can't do with my property. Besides, they don't have room fer all of us in their jail, and they would surely tire of yer caterwaulin', William," Jotham joked. "I'm standin' by you, Eb. I'll do nothin', just like ye."

"We all have to be united in this. We have no means to negotiate. We have to do this together," Mudgett said. He looked around the room. He had convinced Jotham. *Would the others follow?* The silence gave way to shuffling of feet and grunts.

Ebenezer had fanned the embers of discontent. He took in a long breath and waited to see if they caught or he needed to stoke them some more. Suddenly,

Abraham stood up and declared, "Count me in! This damn law has been gettin' on my wick long enough. I won't be payin'!"

Ebenezer exhaled the breath he didn't realize he was holding. The rest of them jumped to their feet, albeit one by one, and echoed Abraham, each more passionate than the one before. The last holdout was Aaron Quimby's brother, Will. Finally, the contagious burst of enthusiasm in the room overwhelmed him, too. He was swept up in the spirited camaraderie. To commit to an ideal made them giddy. It was liberating to respond to the transgressions imposed upon them, like shucking off a heavy coat on a hot day. The act of defiance was forging a tighter bond in their friendship. It was an invisible chain linking them with a common purpose. They were in this together, a brotherhood ready to face what the future would hold, come what may.

Over the course of the following week, the Weare men fanned out and visited the other sawmills listed in the citation. With the fire of resistance still burning in their chests, they preached the sermon of defiance. The sawyers listened. Some were inspired, but when the sawyers conveyed the prospect of intransigence to their neighbors, the embers slowly died. The accused men from other mills cited in the *Gazette* were not convinced that sacrificing all they had struggled to build would deliver anything but disaster to themselves and their families. Perhaps, had Ebenezer been the one to speak with them the outcome would have been different. All but the eight men from Clement's sawmill appeared before Samuel Blodgett, paid the fine, and were free to take their white pine logs. Governor Wentworth declared they had gotten off easy.

A Warrant Is Served

The February snow and ice gave way to the March mud which led to April's soft breezes. The physical change in the environment was pleasant and relaxing for the soul, but it was deceiving; as the rebirth of nature was taking place, the men were getting more and more anxious. Their defiance would not be ignored for long. The dawning of each day brought them closer to the inevitable confrontation.

Ebenezer was afforded months to contemplate his rebellion. As is often the case when time is allowed to stretch, he found himself listening to two voices in his head. One spoke firmly and convincingly about the odious exploitation of their pine trees, coupled with the abuse and threats from the King's representatives. Its manifestation cried for agitation similar to what the Sons of Liberty were doing. The other voice, perhaps not as resolute at first, entered timidly specifying caution, restraint. The counterpoint grew out of fear of reprisals to his family and concern for how they would manage without him. As the period of contemplation increased, and Miriam and his eight children enveloped him in their daily joys, the latter voice grew stronger and drowned out the former. *Dear God, how could I risk putting my family in jeopardy?* He thought. *Perhaps it isn't too late to visit that duplicitous Sam Blodgett and pay the damn fine.* He was ready for it just to be finished. He wondered if he even felt a tinge of relief for his consideration to relent to the King.

Miriam was showing Claire where she had stored the soap—out of reach of William. He had recently discovered how easily the cakes of soap could be carved and, in doing so, had cut his finger. "I know the cut was not deep enough to be an adequate lesson. I suspect he will have another go at it if I don't remove it to a higher shelf." Claire was agreeing.

Ebenezer was searching for some paperwork on his desk. He was confident he had placed the note in question on top of other papers, but perhaps it had been pushed to the side. He was muttering to himself about how the children were always keen on playing around his desk; Claire was never strict enough to stop them. He would have to speak to Miriam about her. It wouldn't hurt to hire a more assertive housemaid.

"Mama, Papa, that man is back! Another one is with him!" Ezra ran into the house shouting. If he didn't understand the man's hidden agenda months before in their home, he remembered the pall that blanketed the room with his presence. Ezra had also heard his name spoken in a hushed whisper, not a happy secret-keeping kind of whisper, one that was pushed out of the mouth as though it were a bad taste. "They are tyin' up their horses now."

Benjamin Whiting found great satisfaction in his job. He was loyal to his King and took the responsibility seriously. Wayward colonists disgusted him. At the thought, he made a sour face as if he had just eaten something vile, and spat on the ground. John Quigley spat, too. Whiting scowled at him. The imitation reflected how unfitting the act was for a royal emissary. Whiting swiftly squared his shoulders. Ebenezer peeked out the window; what he was seeing made him suspect that Whiting was summoning a royal presence as if he dared to embody King George himself. The sheriff relaxed the muscles in his face, exposing his natural scowl, took a deep breath, and raised his head high. Mudgett recognized Whiting was on a royal mission to apprehend and punish a rebellious subject, *him*. Whiting strode to the door with the warrant held in front of him. Quigley followed him like a puppy. He nodded to his deputy and Quigley knocked three times. Whiting smiled. "I am besought with a vision of a family of mice, suddenly startled by a predator, scurrying around in circles, uncertain where to hide,"

he sniffed to his deputy.

Ebenezer appeared at the door. Miriam was within earshot but hidden from view. Ebenezer dispensed with a greeting and instead glared at the sheriff and his deputy.

"Sir, I have in my hand a warrant for yer arrest. Ye have most *egregiously* disobeyed our Majesty . . ."

"King George," John Quigley interrupted. Quigley suddenly felt Benjamin Whiting's hand applying pressure to his upper arm.

"Ye are to bid yer family farewell and come with us," Whiting continued.

Ebenezer lingered. He shifted support from one leg to another. "It is getting late. We will not be able to make the journey before nightfall. I have the right to post bail, do I not?" he asked rhetorically. "I can gather the funds tonight and meet you in the morrow with the bail."

The sheriff was silent for a minute. He turned to Deputy Quigley and hissed, "I told you to be ready to leave for Weare by noon. We would have been here earlier if you had not dillydallied and then offered some weak excuse!" He flashed an angry look in Quigley's direction; the deputy immediately moved back a step.

At the start of their mission, Benjamin Whiting had told Quigley that he wanted nothing more than to make a lesson out of Mudgett and was eager for his arrest; however, he was a pragmatic man. "It is only out of my liberal generosity that I will agree to your proposal. Mark me, I will expect to see the entire bail as listed in this warrant, sir. We shall be waiting fer ye at Quimby's Inn. Ye will experience grave consequences if ye choose to forestall this arrangement." He handed Ebenezer the warrant, bid good day, and pushed Quigley toward the horses.

Earlier in the day, John Quigley had been bragging in the Goat's Head about the warrant he was going to serve Ebenezer. Unbeknownst to him, the tavern held sympathizers for Ebenezer's plight. It wasn't difficult for them to trick Quigley into divulging the details of the warrant and its delivery. Keeping the rum flowing granted them the time and opportunity to apprise others of Ebenezer's reckoning. So it was that half an hour after the two Tories left the Mudgett residence, support rode in from all sections of Weare. Twenty men filled Ebenezer's meeting room, among them were his friends: Abraham Johnson, Timothy and Jonathan Worthley, Caleb Atwood, William Dustin, Will Quimby, Jotham Tuttle, and Samuel Goodale.

"I have bail I can give!" Samuel punched the air with his fist.

"Me too!" another man said slamming his fist into an open hand.

Ebenezer raised his hand to still the various suggestions springing up around the room. His slumped shoulders and downcast look did not resemble the man who had fired them up months before. He had come to a bitter conclusion.

"No, no. I'm done with it all. I will pay the bail and suffer the fate in due time. Go home to yer families and speak with them about this matter. I will surrender and face the consequences. I appreciate . . ."

"Dear friend!' William Dustin interrupted. While fingering his beard, he worked his way through the throng and stood next to Ebenezer. "Ye have disappointed us! What is the matter with ye? Where is the fearless man who encouraged us to resist, who said he would not pay one shilling! Are ye forgettin' the injustice of the Pine Tree Law, the Crown's control over our livelihood? Ye are the one that convinced us to join together against the royal scourge that has infested our land! We have the opportunity to do what ye have been preachin' to us, friend. The time has come to make our frustration known!"

"That's correct!" Abraham added. His wide stance with his hands on his hips showed confidence and determination. "Ye told us to bide our time. The chance would present itself! This is it, Eb, and it's as good as any!"

Amid the ringing affirmations of the men, Jotham shouted, "Look around, Ebenezer! We are not turnin' our backs on ye! We have come to lend ye support! We will not be payin' our fines, come what may."

"This is it! I fer one am ready to show England that we are not goin' to be toleratin' the abuse any longer. Ye told us, Ebenezer, that if we don't show our displeasure of the tree law, they will keep on enforcin' it and add others to it. Well, let them experience our displeasure!" Timothy said.

Jonathan, nodding in agreement with Timothy, cried out, "Ye showed us the articles in *the Massachusetts Spy*, ye spoke of the Sons of Liberty, and *the Massachusett's Circular Letter*. New Hampshire can send a message, too! It is our turn!"

Ebenezer glanced to his left. Miriam, framed by the doorway, was listening to the comments. She met his eyes, shrugged her shoulders, and retreated to the kitchen. He knew that their conversation tonight would repeat what they both had been saying since receiving Sam Blodgett's letter, *there is no easy solution to this puzzle, give in or resist, either way, we are at risk*. He silently wished he could convince her that resistance might be the better option. He turned back to the group and studied their anxious faces.

The enthusiasm to rebel was infectious. Ebenezer felt energy slowly surge through his body. Since the fateful trip to Salem, he had worn himself out trying to instill the rebellious spirit in other settlers. He was never certain if the anarchistic spark had indeed caught. *Talk is no commitment until it has been tested—like now* . . . He drew himself up and shook his head as if shaking off the burden of resignation.

"If ye are indeed with me, then the choice is made! King George will soon learn that the good people of Weare, New Hampshire, will not tolerate his oppression any longer!"

His decisiveness sent cheers up from all parts of the

room. "Be advised, this is treason; we will be opposing the Crown." He paused. "But . . . We will be sendin' a message to like-minded colonists. Our defiance is not a whim. Our defiance is the result of an unjust law that has been repugnant from the start. Whatever action we decide to take, it must be scandalous enough to hasten its gossip throughout the other towns. The more flagrant the act, the wider it will spread. They call us *notorious offenders*, so we shall do something notorious!"

"The sheriff and deputy are expecting ye after sunup," William Dustin said, "so, they'll not be anticipatin' if we *all* show up in the dark hours of early morn."

"True, anything we do must be done on the sly to catch them off-guard," offered Jotham. "But Aaron's not gonna like us chargin' into his inn. Besides, he most likely bolts the door at night."

"That's why we have Will Quimby here!" Caleb laughed. "Will, ye must go over to yer brother's inn and let him know we plan on makin' some noise early tomorrow."

"What kind of noise are we gonna make?" Samuel asked.

"I think the noise will be comin' mostly from Quigley and Whiting," Abraham said.

For an hour they discussed the details of the plan. Most wanted harsh retribution. A few naive souls favored a softer approach, but they were finally won over. The overwhelming agreement was not to mortally wound either man; however, they were going to make them wish the governor had never enforced the Pine Tree Law. The men convinced Will Quimby to go to his brother's inn where the two authorities, Whiting and Quigley, were spending the night. The plan hinged on Will's ability to convince his brother to allow two dozen men to storm inside, where Aaron's wife and children would be sleeping, and beat up the governmental representatives.

Will stared at his brother. He bit his bottom lip and ran his hands up and down the arms of the maple rocker several times. Aaron watched the nervous movement, and a small frown appeared on his brow. "Brother, I am perplexed by this late call and why ye must speak out of earshot of my dear wife, but I suppose if it were serious ye would have blurted it out by this time."

Will inhaled through his nose and held his breath for a second. When he expelled it through his mouth, he was ready to begin. He leaned forward, and in a hushed voice, he slowly enlightened Aaron on the plan taking place in his inn early the next morning.

"Are ye daft, Will? Ye know well that I'm no friend to the Crown, but I've a wife and children to think of, a new-born baby. How can ye promise that no harm will come to them or the inn during the scuffle?"

"Ye'll be showin' me the right room to enter. No one will bother with any other parts. Aaron, ye've been hearin' bitter complaints for years against the tree law. It has affected everybody. This may be the only chance we get to challenge the law and make our resentment known." Will's patient coaxing ultimately weakened Aaron's resolve.

"We need ye to keep the front door unlocked, and I need to know where they'll be sleepin'. Stay in yer bedroom. No one will bother ye, but t'would be best if ye didn't come out, same with the children."

The Pine Tree Riot

Whether one believes that a higher power created man or that he evolved from jungle dwelling primates, most people agree that human beings have free choice. Situations appear regularly that test men's options and values. Periodically, a good man will make, or be forced to make, a difficult choice. Driven to the brink of desperation and hopelessness, he will push beyond the boundaries of his temperament and redefine himself. Certain circumstances can induce a prudent and law-abiding person to perform outside his realm of acceptability. With the hatred for the King and all who represent him steadfastly building, many good men were destined to cross that line. Ebenezer Mudgett and his friends' decision to defy the law, the King, tweaked their characters in such a way they would soon behave in a manner foreign to themselves and all who knew them.

Just before dawn on April 14, 1772, Ebenezer Mudgett was outside Quimby's Inn trembling slightly from the cool air and anticipation. He shifted from foot to foot. He wasn't nervous. He was impatient. *Where are they?* The previous fall's leaves, still wet from yesterday's rain, were spongy beneath his feet. *It's almost dawn. There isn't much time left.* He shifted to a different foot; this time he leaned against a large oak tree. He was a man of action, and once he made a decision, he was eager to move forward.

It was still dark—and quiet. Eb felt a shiver creep up his back as the cold, musty morning air settled all around him. *At least it isn't raining now.* He was beginning to get more and more impatient for the men to arrive. He shifted his weight again. *Did they change their minds?* In a few hours the sun would warm the air and the ground underneath him, but not now. By then, they will have accomplished their deed. He curled his toes away from the dampness creeping into the front of his boots. The plan was to meet in front of Quimby's Inn before sunrise and take Ben Whiting and his deputy, John Quigley, by surprise. *It will be a pleasure to see Whiting's frightened face.*

Suddenly he was aware of movement. The emerging figures were difficult to identify. He could only recognize a few by the way they walked. The lanterns cast eerie dancing lights on their blackened faces. He acknowledged Caleb's voice.

"I've brought bail!" Caleb raised his birch switch over his head and whipped it down.

"Shhh," someone hissed. A few snickered.

He approached the group. "I think he will be

surprised we plan to pay him in full this day!" He raised his lantern to identify Samuel joining the mix. He handed him a chunk of charcoal. "Here, rub this on yer face. T'isn't as good as a mask, but it'll help."

The men tightened their circle around Ebenezer and waited. The anticipation was palpable. They passed a flask of rum from man to man.

"Will said Aaron would leave the door unlocked," Ebenezer whispered.

Light was just beginning to filter through the trees. Ebenezer surveyed the two dozen men assembled near him. "Those of ye with switches follow Will and me. If ye have branches or poles, remain outside in the event they manage to escape. If ye came empty-handed, do as ye choose."

Ebenezer and Will Quimby led the way to the door. No one made a sound in spite of the bumping and jostling to keep their ranks tight. One by one the men with green birch rods slipped inside the building. Will looked at Mudgett and pointed to the bedroom his brother had shown him earlier. Benjamin Whiting and John Quimby would be sleeping inside. Ebenezer nodded. The men held back to wait for his signal. He crept toward the door. A floorboard squeaked. As though that were the call for his action, Ebenezer threw the door open and entered the room alone.

"I'm here to give my bail!" he shouted.

The sheriff had been lost in a deep, satisfying sleep; the abrupt awakening confused and startled him. Instinctively, he grabbed the quilt and clutched it against his chest. He squinted and frowned in the direction of the apparition, trying to focus and decipher the significance of its words. A few seconds later he registered the purpose of the intrusion. He tightened his lips in deprecation and responded with a characteristic growl.

"Mudgett! Damnation, could ye not have waited fer the sun to rise any higher!" He whipped the quilt back and sat on the edge of the bed. "Yer dear wife must have thrown ye outta yer damn bed. Who could blame her!" He was still cursing as he stood to stretch out his muscles and pull on his trousers.

When he started to reach for his shirt, Ebenezer gave a loud whoop. Ten men came charging into the room, switches held high, yelling and shouting. Quigley, confounded by Mudgett's early entrance, had been sitting up in his bed. He hollered. Whiting immediately grabbed his pistols. Five men lunged across his bed and intercepted him. Whiting would have shot as many intruders as possible if not for the struggle that ensued. They wrenched the pistols from his hands. Someone pushed his face down against the pine floor. He thrashed about, but several bodies had pinned him down. His cheek flattened against the floorboard.

Several aggressors flew across the room to apprehend the horrified deputy. He let out an anguished wail but managed to grab a small bedside table. He was backed against a wall, sliding himself toward the corner of the room and frantically swinging the table to keep the men at bay. The switches whipped at the table, unable to reach him. The blackened faces were jeering at him.

"Ye will regret this! I am the sheriff of this county! Ye will not get away with this!" Whiting boomed from the other side of the room. "I'll have ye all drawn 'n quartered!"

"Grab his other leg!"

"Each take an arm! Lift him up!"

"He's a heavy louse!"

They hoisted him up; two men on each side managed to keep him steady despite his desperate attempts to wiggle loose.

"T'was the bail ye wanted? Here it is!" One of the men started the flogging, and two others joined in. Each swing registered the injustice for each log cut, drawn, and forfeited.

John Quigley was still controlling the small knot of men and attempting to inch his way toward the door. He emitted little yelps of pain as the switches whipped at his hands and legs.

Outside, a few of the restless men were thumping their poles into the wet earth and getting impatient. One of them announced, "Why should they have all the fun. Some of you keep watch out here in case they escape. I'm goin' in!" Five men followed him.

The six assailants stampeded into the inn and ran in the direction of the brawl. It was evident from Whiting's wailing that he was well taken care of. Quigley, however, was still managing to avoid capture. Deciding they might have a better vantage point from a higher level, they ran up toward the garret. Some remained on the stairs and held their poles like spears, ready to thrust them at any moment. The ones without poles ran to the room above the scuffle. They managed to pry up some loose floorboards and peered down. Quigley was wedged in a corner, thus protected from a rear attack. His head became the target of their improvised weapons. His cry was a mixture of surprise and pain. His only means of escape would be out the bedroom door. He inched along the wall, dodging the boards and whips as best he could. As soon as he backed through the bedroom's doorframe, the men on the stairs sent their poles sailing though the air. Their target let out a howl. His attention was immediately diverted from the birch rods in front of him to the heavy ash poles jabbing him in his back and head. He dropped the table and fell to the floor. He folded himself up like a hedgehog but didn't have the luxury of the same spiny protection. The men coming down the stairs scooped him up. Someone threw the table out into the hall, smashing it. Four men grabbed Quigley's arms and legs and dragged him into the room, treating him to the same reward Benjamin Whiting was suffering.

Meanwhile, Aaron Quimby had reluctantly followed his brother's instructions to stay in his bedroom and to lock his children in their rooms. Will had made him promise not to leave his room—no matter what he heard outside his door. Aaron would tell his brother later that that was the hardest thing for him to do. The sounds of men running and furniture crashing caused his wife to bolt upright and scream. She grabbed onto folds of his nightshirt; if there had been any light in the room, he would have seen the terror in her eyes. It was only then that he confided what was transpiring in their inn. If she had known in advance, the plan surely would have been jeopardized.

Outside, the rest of the men were eager to participate. They relished playing a bigger part in the agitation; after all, some of them were notorious offenders, too. They bandied around their ideas about what to do when the Tories finally emerged.

"Perhaps there might be something in Aaron's shed we could use," Will suggested. Samuel joined him behind the inn to investigate.

They opened the thin pine door as wide as it would allow. The meager light from the early sun fell on the rim of a metal receptacle.

"A bucket of whitewash. T'would be good ta cover up the lashings, give 'em a nice white coat that's none too easy to remove!" Samuel ventured deeper inside with Will at his back. His eyes tried to adjust to the dim light before he could identify what lay around them.

Samuel stooped down and found a pair of shears. "These might be handy."

Will spotted two empty metal pails. "T'would be nice to make some music for the ole boys, give 'em a nice send-off!"

"I can't see much else in here."

They started to leave when Will's foot kicked a small tin horn. He picked it up and inspected it. "One of my nephews must 'a been in here pokin' around and left his little horn here." He blew in it.

"Bless me, Will! Ye sound like a sheep squeezin' out a lamb!"

The two carried their new-found materials back to the men waiting outside the house, who were starting to get unruly. Two of them had been running back and forth to yell reports on the activities inside. The others were running around the inn to ensure neither one of their marks would escape. Samuel set the bucket of whitewash near the door. A few men eagerly joined them to see what they had found.

"I didn't find a paintbrush. I guess we can dump this on 'em."

One of the men saw the shears in Will's pile. He picked them up, walked over to the horses, and said gaily over his shoulder, "Don't fret, Samuel. Perhaps I could make one!"

He stood to the side of Whiting's black horse, raised the beautiful long tail, and smiled back at the others. The horse was startled by the touch but didn't kick. He dropped the shears and held the liberated tail high. He smiled and draped it over his head. It fell on either side of his face. Fluttering his eyes, he said in a high-pitched voice, "Where is my dear husband? Benjamin! Come to bed!" The other men laughed.

One of them joked, "This might be the only way ye can get someone in yer bed. Ye look fairly appealin'!" The man quickly removed it and whipped it in a circle. He barked a laugh and went over to the pail of lime and water. He draped one end into the bucket and swirled it around.

Another man went over to the horses. He picked up the shears. He studied the dappled horse's white tail. He smiled and said, "I conclude one paintbrush is not enough." He held the tail tightly in his left hand and snipped it short like the other. "Might as well be sure to decrease their value as well," and he clipped the frightened animal's ears. It took three men to hold the horse from bolting.

The first group of men emerged from the inn.

"Let all know; the bail is paid in full!" Abraham yelled.

The last to come out were the ones struggling to carry the sheriff and his deputy. The dead weight caused Caleb to stumble, but he quickly righted himself. Timothy and Jonathan Worthley led the frantic horses to the front of the house. By this time, another zealous marauder had cleaned each horse of its mane.

Samuel smeared the whitewash on Whiting's naked back. The white started to turn pink. The pressure and roughness of the wiry horsehair on his inflamed back caused him to arch his back and groan.

"I'll have ye all thrown in prison. The governor will make ye suffer." His muffled voice had lost its strength and could barely be heard above the taunts.

Ebenezer and Abraham had already hoisted Quigley, facing backward, onto his horse. He was hunched over and whimpering. Someone had generously applied whitewash on his painful lacerations, and little pink and red streams were running down his pants and pooling on the ground.

"Let's get the *good gentleman* on his steed," Jotham said sarcastically. Jotham and another man heaved Whiting up backward as well. His horse buckled a bit under the sudden weight. Timothy stood in front of the horse and held the reins close to the bit, pulling downwards to prevent him from bolting. Both horses were protesting and trying to shake loose. Their equally nervous riders were bounced back and forth as the horses pivoted around Timothy and Jonathan, who were desperately trying to keep them still.

Two men had found sticks and were beating the bottoms of the empty buckets. They were laughing and striking them with different rhythms. Will Quimby leaned back, and with knees slightly bent and head raised, he took a deep breath and blew into the tin horn. The strange bleating-toots sent gales of laughter into the misty air.

Timothy nodded at his brother, and both let go of the reins and jumped aside. Someone slapped the horses' rumps. They raised their stubbed tails, shifted their weight to their haunches, and with their front legs raised, pushed off. Whiting and Quigley had to lean back toward their horses' necks to avoid falling off, but then they were propelled forward toward the rumps. With pounding hooves, the horses bounced the sorry figures down the road heading south. The men with instruments ran after them, serenading them until the horses were out of sight. Several curious townspeople were visible in the distance, having been told in advance of the plot and eager to see if the men were successful.

Ebenezer watched them disappear. "I believe we will succeed in being notorious tonight. They shall have to explain the stripes on their backs, and although I do not favor ridding the horses of the means to swipe away the flies, their appearance will serve to help spread the rumor." He felt a flutter of pride thinking the man in Salem would have approved of their nasty deed.

Retribution Expected

"Ye wanted agitation, friend, and agitation we gave!" Caleb shouted. The adrenalin was still running high, and the men met the announcement with a loud round of cheering and hooting. The agitators clapped each other on the back and laughed.

"Whiting and Quigley know what offenders we are now!"

Will raised his hand to attract attention. "Now, let us tell my brother . . . his guests slipped out without payin' fer their room!" he spit out laughing. There was no reaction from the men. Instead, they were looking beyond him. He turned in the direction of their stares to face the front door of the inn. His grin froze for a second and then slowly withered.

Standing in the doorway was his sister-in-law, Anna, gripping a shawl around herself in one hand and shaking a broken table piece in the other. Wide-eyed children were trembling and grabbing at her nightgown or peering from around her back. The reprimands issuing from her hoarse voice were not nearly as sinister as her appearance. Will had never seen her hair unpinned. The wavy, gray-streaked tresses blowing in the wind and the furious, squinty-eyed glare sent a shiver up his back.

Ebenezer and the others felt like schoolboys being chastised and made to reflect on their misconduct. Eb glanced around at the overturned buckets, the white liquid splashed everywhere, and the horsehair scattered like hay around the yard. Some of the men cleared their throats and shifted their stances, but most stood stock still. When Anna exhausted her chiding, she threw the table fragment down and stomped back into the inn, dragging the children. Ebenezer could hear Aaron's muffled pleas for her to calm down amid the wailing of the youngest children. He could tell the innkeeper was not succeeding.

Ebenezer broke the silence on the lawn. "We must hurry. Ye know how that bastard is. It won't take long for Whiting to demand that a posse come lookin' fer us. They know exactly who to look fer. Get yourselves to yer homes, grab some provisions, and find a place to hide in the woods for a few days. I'll be hidin' where the giant boulders rest on each other, where we go to camp while huntin'."

Within minutes the men fled to their homes, leaving Aaron alone to defend himself against the remonstrations of his wife. Ebenezer's last look before running to his house was Aaron working his way around the yard picking up the evidence of the episode. Anna was following and sputtering with every footstep. He hoped Aaron would be able to explain that the growing acrimony they all felt from the royal subjugation justified the punishment. If not, it would be a long time before he would be welcome back at their inn.

A small crowd of villagers was afforded the pleasure of witnessing the spectacle of the two miserable officials bouncing backward out of town. The news of their embroilment had spread, and despite the early hour, a gauntlet was ready and waiting. They were ushered out of town amid cheers and insults, adding to their humiliation.

When the horses slowed down, the men managed to twist themselves back around in their saddles, but they could not conceal their chastened aspects. At first glance, no one identified Whiting. He had lost the two qualities that a casual observer, even from afar, first registered with him: his regal posture and pompous air. John Quigley was also not recognized at first glance. It was inconceivable to associate the arrogant men with the maimed, degraded ones that rode by on their disgraced horses. An old man approaching them from the opposite direction stood transfixed and perplexed by the duo. His head tilted as if to ask what they had done to deserve such punishment. A few children they encountered were bold enough to ask what their parents did not dare, "What happened to you? Why are your horses free of their tails and manes? Did you cut their ears?" They received no comment from either man. A couple of spectators along the route, overcome by curiosity, ran closer to scrutinize the pair. They finally discerned Whiting by his most unmistakeable feature: the ever-present scowl. John Quigley was bent over to hide his shame but was unable to hide his face.

Word of the surprise attack on the sheriff and his deputy traveled quickly from tavern to tavern. Additionally, the ones who had seen the woeful figures were eager to spread their gossip. Many who had been on the losing end of Whiting's wrath and Quigley's disparagement were pleased to hear of their mortification. Within a week's time, the Pine Tree Riot was common knowledge—not only in Weare but the surrounding towns as well.

As expected, Benjamin Whiting and John Quigley's outrage and embarrassment from the degrading and painful experience caused them to seek reprisal immediately. Whiting expressed his fervent desire to give the men a taste of martial law. He chose his revenge by enlisting the aid of Colonel John Goffe of Deerfield and Colonel Edward Goldstone Lutwytche of Merrimack. The soldiers agreed to send a posse from their two regiments. On April 16th the militia, outfitted with muskets, marched into Weare. On April 17th the foiled soldiers returned. It seemed the King's coveted pines in the thick Weare woods had successfully helped to conceal the fugitives. Nevertheless, Whiting's honor and reputation were at stake, and he was not going to allow the offense to go unpunished.

"I was almost killed! The rioters assaulted me, the

Sheriff of the County. They not only caused me considerable pain but they disparaged the Office of Sheriff! They disgraced the King! I will not allow this matter to rest!" Whiting blustered to the supporters he had gathered. He encouraged the small group to fan out in Weare, listen in taverns, and spy around the rioters' homes. "It will only be a matter of time before they will be apprehended, and they will be apprehended!" he bellowed, arching his painful back away from the rough linen shirt.

Samuel was accustomed to living in the woods, but the meadow brook's cool water did little to alleviate his thirst for ale. That and the merciless early blackflies had weakened his reserve. He had spent most of his time waving an empty grain sack around his head to keep the tiny flies from attaching around his ears. Instead, the tenacious gnats crawled up his moose-hide trousers to suck his blood and leave nasty, itchy welts.

"I need to get myself some ale or cider. T'wouldn't hurt to sneak outta here fer a bit tonight. Maybe I can get some news," he mumbled to himself. He yanked up his pant leg and scratched furiously.

Samuel waited until dusk to work his way out of the woods. Once he got on the north road, he let the smoke issuing from the chimneys guide him to Mudgett's house. Someone there would be able to give him word as to what to do next. More importantly, his stomach was telling him he needed something to eat. His meager rations had not lasted long.

The night was too dark for him to see the man sitting under Ebenezer's tree. He had been there, day and night, for several days. Whiting had threatened all his supporters that he sent to Weare not to return without a captive. This man was about to get himself a prisoner.

Samuel stumbled in the dark and instinctively swore.

"Who goes there?"

Samuel froze. The man rose and walked gingerly to where he had heard the sound. The vigilante, detecting the shape of a man, lunged at him. He knocked Samuel over. Samuel had just enough time to roll away before the man drew his gun. He was scrambling away on his hands and knees when the gun went off.

"Stop right there, or the next bullet will find ye!"

Within seconds, Moses bounded out of the house, swinging a lantern as he ran. He recognized Samuel and relief spread across his face—his father must still be safe. The man grabbed the lantern from Moses and held it up to Samuel's face. Black remnants of charcoal were evident around his eyes and forehead.

"I think ye'll be comin' with me tonight." He restrained Samuel's hands behind his back and led him across the street to Quimby's. Anna Quimby's stern countenance frightened Samuel almost as much as being held captive. The next day Samuel would find himself in jail.

Moses ran back to the house. His mother met him at the door. She had heard the shot and feared the worst.

"It wasn't father," he said resting his hand on her shoulder. She closed her eyes and drew a deep breath of relief. "Somehow I need to get word to him, Mother."

Early the next day Moses woke, grabbed his rifle, and headed to the woods. If anyone questioned him, he would say he was going hunting. With any luck, he might be able to return with an animal to show for it. Nevertheless, he periodically looked over his shoulder to be certain no one was following him. He headed to where he had an idea his father might be hiding.

The Ice Age had liberally deposited granite rocks throughout New Hampshire. Most of them had been crushed in transit and had significantly reduced in size, but a couple of giant boulders on Mudgett's land had been left to stand as testimony to the power of frozen water. Moss and lichen adorned their rough exterior; fragrant evergreens concealed the cave. Their juxtaposition made it possible for a man to crawl inside the created cavity and disappear from view. It would not be the most comfortable place to spend several nights, but desperation feeds willpower.

Moses headed for the massive rock formation where he used to play—a time before he was needed to help with the chores. It was also a time when he did not have to compete for his father's attention. His closest live sibling was Sarah, four years his junior. In their time alone, Ebenezer had taught him some birdcalls. He had explained to Moses that this was how the Indians used to communicate in the forest, a secret language that filtered through the trees. Moses never mastered them, but the two always had a good laugh with the imitations. It was years ago when he last tried to produce their calls. He started with a robin's chirping. The result was no better than when he was four. He walked a few feet, turned his head in different directions, and attempted more. His pathetic rendering was too weak to carry more than a meager distance. The only other call he could remember was the barn owl. The screeching sound traveled farther. Every few minutes, Moses would put his head back, position his hands on either side of his mouth, and screech.

"Are ye tryin' to wake the dead, Son?" Grinning broadly, Ebenezer emerged from behind a pine's solid trunk.

"Father, they caught Samuel Goodale."

With provisions replenished by family members, the fugitives waited several more days in the forests. When they sensed that the commotion had died down and Whiting's supporters had given up and deserted the frustrated sheriff, they trickled out. Word reached them to meet at Mudgett's.

"Friends, we have made our resistance public. The good people of this town and beyond have had little else to gossip about these past weeks. I have heard that Whiting himself cannot refrain from spewing his anger to all he meets! We have accomplished our mission." Ebenezer had been trying to explain the same to Miriam since he returned but was experiencing more luck with his comrades.

"What will become of ye? They will surely put all of ye away like Samuel." Miriam addressed the group. Her arms slapped her sides in frustration.

William Dustin approached her, "Now, we will go to Samuel Blodgett and pay the bail. Young Samuel will be set free. Then we will wait our fate. We have the stirring of sentiment in our favor. I hear we have been toasted and cheered in many establishments. We shall not allow this fervor to die." Miriam responded with a sigh of resignation. William's understated tone did little to assuage her uneasiness. She left them to raise their mugs and relive their audacity, growing in daring and heroic measures.

When the men left, Miriam confronted her husband again. "I simply do not understand yer gaiety, husband! Ye have committed a lawless act against the Sheriff of the County performin' his legal responsibility—for *the King!* I am astounded ye think so lightly of yer act and what the future holds!"

Ebenezer attempted once again to explain, knowing that he would nonetheless never convince her that their action against the officials was warranted. "What we did was to take a stand, Miriam. It might be called drastic by some, but it would not have carried on the wind as far as it has if we had merely used words. We will face the consequences knowing that our agitation had some results, we started a conversation that has been repeated from tavern to tavern."

Jesse wandered by, indifferent to the same heated conversation that had been commonplace for days. Eb was grateful for the interruption. He scooped him up and flung him onto his shoulders. Ebenezer was dancing in a tight circle, bouncing the delighted child, who would certainly have fallen off if not for Ebenezer holding onto his son's little legs. Miriam had to shout over the gales of laughter.

"Enjoy their laughter whilst ye can, husband." She flashed her husband a look mixed with concern and uncertainty. Ebenezer was confident his optimism would eventually win her over. He had five months to try until the court date. *Perhaps she would feel differently if she could hear the support I am hearing in the taverns,* he thought.

September 8, 1772

The Superior Court of Judicature in Amherst was stifling. The September air could not compete with the combined heat of the bodies that were packed shoulder to shoulder like closed fingers on a hand. People had been waiting for months to hear the verdict on the men who had dared to attack and humiliate the sheriff. The line outside His Majesty's Superior Court had begun to form an hour before the doors opened. When they were flung open, men and women did not wait their turns but squeezed through the doorframe together, some getting momentarily stuck until one was able to wedge sideways.

The accused were sitting in the front row, cautiously encouraged by the number of supporters pouring inside to fill both floors of the building. The chief justice, the Honorable Theodore Atkinson, frowned as he attempted to stifle the jittery chattering. His wooden gavel was on its fifth repetition of pounding before the noise finally subsided. Seated on his right were the honorable justices: Meshech Weare, Leverett Hubbard, and William Parker. They wore long black robes and tightly curled wigs perched on their heads. Ebenezer was concerned about their inclinations toward the case; not one had returned his glance. Benjamin Whiting, having healed from his lacerations and sitting straight-backed, was wearing the expression of a wounded man deserving retribution.

Justice Atkinson pounded his gavel on the block one more time and nodded to a tall, thin man off on the side. The man nodded and stepped forward. The crowd started to hush.

"Anno Regui Regis Georgii Tertii. God save the King." The multitude responded without much enthusiasm, "God save the King."

While Justice Atkinson droned on about the formality of the procedure and the respect due the justices and their decisions, Ebenezer was wondering if he had been foolish to feel optimistic. He looked at Meshech Weare. He was an imposing statesman. *Was it a disadvantage that their town was named after him? Would he be insulted and think that they had disgraced the name?* He didn't have time to dwell on the answers.

"Timothy Worthley, Jonathan Worthley, Caleb Atwood, William Dustin, Abraham Johnson, Jotham Tuttle, William Quimby, Samuel Goodale, and Ebenezer Mudgett. You are charged with being rioters, routers, disturbers of the peace and with making an assault upon the body of Benjamin Whiting, Sheriff. And that you beat, wounded and evilly treated him among other injuries, and in doing so, his life was despaired of, he being in execution of his office, against the peace of our Lord the King, his Crown and dignity."

Whiting nodded his head in acknowledgment as Chief Justice Atkinson read each travesty committed against him.

At the chief justice's mention of *assault upon the body*, someone in the back of the room started to snicker. Subsequent chortles initiated a chain reaction throughout the courthouse. Atkinson's voice grew progressively louder as he read the complaint over the laughter in the room. He angrily beat the gavel on its block.

"Silence! Remember this is a court of law!" he shouted. "If ye can not grant it the respect it deserves, we shall close the doors with the lot of ye on the other side!"

Whiting twisted in his seat and scanned the assemblage. The outrage reddened his face and neck. His lips pursed in annoyance.

The justice resumed the proceedings in his regular tone.

"How do ye plead?"

Ebenezer stood. He looked down the row of his fellow offenders. They returned his glance, expressionless. He surveyed the room of expectant faces.

"Guilty, yer Honor."

The courtroom exploded with shouting and cheering.

Judge Atkinson pounded the gavel. "Silence! For the final time, I demand silence!"

He leaned over to confer with the other judges. There was not a sound or a whisper in the courtroom. The people were leaning forward and straining to hear the hushed conversation, nobody more than the accused. Justice Hubbard was expressing his opinion and shaking his head. Ebenezer knew that he was in disagreement with whatever the other judges thought. Justice Weare rapidly scribbled on a piece of paper. He passed it to Justice Parker who read it and passed it to Chief Justice Atkinson. They each nodded, and the chief justice directed a comment at Justice Hubbard. He lifted one eyebrow, paused, and finally appeared to acquiesce.

"Will the accused please stand." There was a sound of wood sliding against wood as the men pushed back their chairs. "Repeat after me, *I plead that I will not contend with our Lord the King but will submit myself to his grace.*" Various levels of masculine voices repeated the plea.

"Therefore, this court orders each of ye to pay a fine of . . . twenty shillings plus costs of prosecution." He quickly pounded the gavel on the block.

Samuel turned to Ebenezer and whispered, "Is that *all*?" Ebenezer was shaking his bowed head in relief and grinning up at the young man. The other men looked at each other in shock and then began to laugh. The crowd cheered louder than before. The men's wives had to push and worm their way through the throng of people to hug their husbands. Miriam was overcome with emotion and relief and took a few minutes to compose herself before she finally navigated through the crowd to Ebenezer.

"Well, husband, let us get home. We have a family waiting for the good news," she smiled up at him, and he returned the gesture with a hug that gripped her as if he were hanging on for dear life. It was finally over.

Sheriff Benjamin Whiting was furious. There was no available outlet or sympathetic ear to expel his fury, so he just slipped away. If he had had a tail, it would have been between his legs.

The punishment for such a great outrage on the Sheriff of the County was slight. The light fine revealed that the judges held more sympathy for the men than they held for the sheriff and the Pine Tree Law. The penalty was especially profound: Theodore Atkinson served on his Majesty's Council, and Meshech Weare and William Parker were members of the House of Representatives. Each had pledged their allegiance to the King by means of their appointments.

The bold men, led by Ebenezer Mudgett, a liquor merchant from a small town in New Hampshire, helped to weave the fabric that defines the American spirit: man's desire to control his own destiny. Like a quilt pieced together from bits of cloth, daring groups of men helped to accomplish independence. They rose up against injustice, oppression, and the lack of representation in the British Parliament to enable the change they needed. Successful resistance required a unified effort. Other Patriots' daring acts in the colonies inspired them and showed them they were not alone in their frustration. The collective sentiment to resist and rebel rose to the surface when it was clear that they had more to lose than their lives; they would be putting their families' futures in peril. Man's innate construction to preserve what is rightfully his and fight to protect those he loves provided the catalyst for them to perform outside their normal modes of behavior. The frustration with the Crown had been building, providing the Weare men with the courage to resist against it. The resentment even inhabited the King's own adjudicators, providing the men with a blanket of protection they did not realize they had. Just as other daring acts inspired the Pine Tree Riot, one can argue that their bold escapade contributed to the necessary motivation for the Boston Tea Party the following year. In part, we may owe our independence from British dominance to the Weare rebels as well as the courageous men who dared to throw the tea into the Boston Harbor. Ebenezer Mudgett and his team of rioters proved that without resistance change cannot occur.

Afterword

Many of the characters and places in *Ebenezer Mudgett and the Pine Tree Riot* are historical. The only fictional characters are Charles, the black ex-slave, John Quigley's brother, Willy, and Nathaniel, who abandoned William Reed at the ferry landing. The most important fictional character is Samuel Goodale. The River Bend Inn and Goat's Head Tavern and their proprietors and wives are also fictitious.

Ebenezer Mudgett died in 1784 after serving in the American Revolution. He swore he would not pay one more shilling to the Crown, and in fact, he and the others did not. In 1976 members of the Weare Junior Historical Society with their adviser and current owner of Ebenezer's house, Arnold Rocklin-Weare, sent twenty shillings to Sir Peter Ramsbotham, the British Ambassador in Washington, DC, to pay for the longstanding lien on the house. Sir Peter replied that all was forgiven, and in deference to the Bicentennial, suggested the money be given to charity.

Miriam Mudgett remarried after Ebenezer's death. She and Ebenezer had eleven surviving children.

Benjamin Whiting met further embarrassment. At the start of the American Revolution, he was banished from his hometown, Hollis, and his property was confiscated. He escaped to Nova Scotia. He left his wife and family behind to fend for themselves.

John Quigley also escaped to Nova Scotia.

John Sherburn disappeared from record.

Samuel Goodale is the only fictional character among the Weare men. William Little's History of Weare tells us that one unidentified man was captured and thrown in jail after the riot. It made sense to choose him. He also helped to provide some background to the King's White Pine Tree Law and the emerging inspections.

Caleb Atwood had distinguished himself as a soldier in the French and Indian War. After the Pine Tree Riot, he became one of Weare's Minutemen and fought in the American Revolution, becoming a lieutenant by war's end. He served at Fort Ticonderoga.

Aaron Quimby served in the war at the Siege of St. John, the outlet of Lake Champlain in Canada. Aaron rose up the ranks to captain.

William Quimby moved to Sandwich, NH.

William Dustin had also fought in the French and Indian War. Like Caleb, he served at Fort Ticonderoga during the Revolution and signed on as a member of the First Committee of Safety. In the spring of 1774 the New Hampshire General Court formed the committee to stem British oppression. He eventually became a lieutenant. It is true that Little recorded he had the only slave, and people actually believed his wife was a witch.

Timothy Worthley became a lieutenant in the Revolution and signed the First Committee of Safety, a committee designed to stem the tide of British oppression. He and his wife had eleven children.

Jonathan Worthley also fought in the Revolution and was in the NH Regiment of Rangers. He served in Captain Aaron Quimby's company. He and his wife had fourteen children.

Abraham Johnson moved around Weare and ended his days on the east side of the Piscataquog River. He was Weare's first hog-reeve, a hog constable charged with the prevention or appraising of damages by stray swine. It was his job to yoke and ring hogs running loose in Weare. The job came to be viewed as a joke, and all newly married men were elected to the position.

Jotham Tuttle was the youngest of the "notorious offenders." He eventually married the Worthley brothers' sister, Molly, and they had eight children.

Samuel Blodgett switched alliances again and was not labeled a Tory. He seemingly left governmental life and opened a store in Goffstown in April 1775. In June 1775 he was connected with the commissary department of the Continental Army.

Governor John Wentworth fled New Hampshire on the eve of the Revolution, and his 6,000-acre summer estate in Wolfeboro was seized and later sold at auction.

Meshech Weare was a leader in framing the constitution in New Hampshire, which was adopted on January 1, 1776, the first state to do so. He was the first constitutional governor, then known as a president, and led New Hampshire as the first state to declare its independence.

Glossary

Bannock – A flat, round bread cooked from grain. (Celtic origin)

Boston Massacre – A street fight that occurred on March 5, 1770, between a "patriot" mob, throwing snowballs, stones, and sticks, and a squad of British soldiers. It resulted in 5 dead patriots, and 6 injuries.

Cricket table – A three-legged table of the Jacobean period

Flip – A warm drink made with West India rum, pieces of pumpkin, apple skins, and bran. A half mug cost three pence.

French and Indian War – It began in 1754 when twenty-two-year old George Washington led Virginia militiamen in an ambush against a French patrol. Fighting ensued on account of a dispute over the confluence of rivers in Ohio and the site of French Fort Duquesne within present-day Pittsburgh, Pennsylvania. The war took place between Virginia and Newfoundland. British and British colonists fought the French and their Indian allies until the war ended in 1763. Some Indian tribes also supported the British.

Goad – A sharp pointed stick used to urge cattle, etc.

Hogshead – a large cask, especially one containing from 63 to 140 gallons (238 to 530 liters).

Loggerhead – A ball or bulb of iron with a long handle kept at a white heat to warm liquids.

Loyalist – a person who remained loyal to the British during the American Revolution; Tory.

Patriot – a person who loves, supports, and defends his or her country and its interests with devotion, and who may regard himself or herself as a defender, especially of individual rights, against presumed interference.

Pence – the plural of penny

Pound – Currency formerly equal to 20 shillings or 240 pence: equal to 100 new pence after decimalization in Feb. 1971. Symbol: £.

Pung – A sleigh with a box-like body

Quartering Act – A requirement for colonists to provide the British soldiers with any needed accommodations or housing. It also required colonists to provide food for any British soldiers in the area.

Rod – A unit of measure; one rod equals approximately 16.5 feet

Shilling – the 20th part of a pound, equal to 12 pence

Tavern vs Inn – Generally, but not always, a tavern in the 18th century served alcohol, but did not accept lodgers; whereas, an inn did both.

Tory – A person who supported the British cause in the American Revolution; a Loyalist.

Townshend Acts – Five Acts with the Revenue Act being the most bothersome. It required the colonists to pay for British imports that had been made with materials from the colonies. It was repealed in 1770 after the Boston Massacre.

Writ of Assistance – Authorization given to British soldiers to search merchandise, homes, and personal property with the excuse of looking for contraband.

Made in United States
Troutdale, OR
10/13/2024